Published by
Laurence King Publishing Ltd
361–373 City Road
London EC1V 1LR
Tel +44 20 7841 6900
E enquiries@laurenceking.com
www.laurenceking.com

A catalogue record for this book is available from the British Library.

ISBN 978-1-7862-7370-3
Designed by John Round Design
Printed in China

Laurence King Publishing is committed to ethical and sustainable
production. We are proud participants in The Book Chain Project®
bookchainproject.com

p.10 *Zollverein School of Management and Design*, SANAA, Essen
p.52 *Wainwright Building*, Adler & Sullivan, St. Louis
p.162 *Royal Palace*, architect unknown, Fez
p.190 *Guggenheim Museum*, Frank Gehry, Bilbao

THE SHORT STORY OF ARCHITECTURE

A Pocket Guide to Key Styles, Buildings, Elements & Materials

Susie Hodge

Laurence King Publishing

Contents

6 Introduction
9 How to use this book

STYLES

12 Ancient Egyptian
13 Pre-Columbian
14 Ancient Greek
15 Buddhist
16 Ancient Roman
17 Byzantine
18 Japanese
19 Hindu
20 Islamic
21 Kalinga
22 Moorish
23 Khmer
24 Romanesque
25 Gothic
26 Renaissance
27 Mughal
28 Palladian
29 Baroque
30 Rococo
31 Neoclassical
32 Gothic Revival
33 Shaker
34 Chicago School
35 Arts and Crafts
36 Art Nouveau
37 Modernist
38 Organic
39 Futurist
40 Expressionist
41 De Stijl
42 International Style
43 Bauhaus
44 Art Deco
45 Geodesic
46 Brutalist
47 Postmodern
48 Minimalist
49 High-tech
50 Sustainable
51 Deconstructivist

THE BUILDINGS

54 *Great Pyramid*
56 *Parthenon*, Ictinus, Callikrates and Phidias
58 *Sanchi Stupa*
60 *Pantheon*
62 *Hagia Sophia*, Isidore and Anthemius
64 *Temple of Inscriptions*
68 *Dome of the Rock*, Raja ibn Haywah and Yazid ibn Sallam
70 *Prambanan*
72 *Maria Laach Abbey*
74 *Angkor Wat*
76 *Krak des Chevaliers*
78 *Chartres Cathedral*
80 *Alhambra*
82 *Santa Maria del Fiore*, Arnolfo di Cambio and Filippo Brunelleschi
86 *Doge's Palace*, Filippo Calendario
88 *Temple of the Sun*
90 *Saint Peter's Basilica*, Donato Bramante and Michelangelo Buonarroti
92 *Shibam*
94 *Saint Basil's Cathedral*, Barma and Postnik Yakovlev
96 *Villa La Rotonda*, Andrea Palladio
98 *Taj Mahal*, Ustad Ahmad Lahori
100 *Rinshunkaku*
102 *Palace of Versailles*, Louis Le Vau and Jules Hardouin-Mansart
106 *Saint Paul's Cathedral*, Christopher Wren
108 *Wieskirche*, Dominikus Zimmermann and Johann Baptist Zimmermann
110 *Hancock Shaker Village*
112 *Capitol Building*, William Thornton and Thomas Ustick Walter
114 *Palace of Westminster*, Charles Barry and Augustus Pugin
116 *Red House*, Philip Webb and William Morris

118 *Neuschwanstein Castle*, Eduard Riedel and Georg von Dollmann
120 *Sagrada Família*, Antoni Gaudí
122 *Wainwright Building*, Louis Sullivan and Dankmar Adler
124 *Karlsplatz Underground Station*, Otto Wagner
126 *Great Mosque of Djenné*, Ismaila Traoré
128 *Rietveld Schröder House,* Gerrit Rietveld
130 *Bauhaus Building*, Walter Gropius
132 *Chrysler Building*, William Van Alen
134 *Villa Savoye*, Le Corbusier and Pierre Jeanneret
138 *Fallingwater*, Frank Lloyd Wright
140 *Seagram Building*, Ludwig Mies van der Rohe
142 *Sydney Opera House*, Jørn Utzon
144 *Cathedral of Brasilia*, Oscar Niemeyer
146 *Habitat 67*, Moshe Safdie
148 *Montreal Biosphere*, Buckminster Fuller
150 *Pompidou Centre*, Richard Rogers and Renzo Piano
152 *Portland Building*, Michael Graves
154 *Vitra Fire Station*, Zaha Hadid
156 *Moriyama House*, Ryue Nishizawa
158 *Bosco Verticale*, Stefano Boeri Architetti
160 *Elbphilharmonie*, Herzog & de Meuron

ELEMENTS
164 Wall
165 Ceiling
166 Door
167 Window
168 Roof
169 Chimney
170 Balcony
171 Arcade
172 Dome
173 Arch
174 Tower
175 Courtyard
176 Staircase

177 Column
178 Buttress
179 Gable
180 Atrium
181 Moulding
182 Nave
183 Vault
184 Spire
185 Minaret
186 Portico/Porch
187 Terrace
188 Piloti
189 Cantilever

MATERIALS
192 Stone
193 Mud-brick/Adobe
194 Bitumen
195 Brick
196 Wood
197 Paper
198 Tiles
199 Bamboo
200 Marble
201 Concrete
202 Wattle and Daub
203 Plaster
204 Mosaic
205 Stucco
206 Glass
207 Stained Glass
208 Iron
209 Steel
210 Aluminium
211 Plastic
212 Carbon Fibre
213 Recycled Materials
214 Composite Materials
215 Titanium

216 Glossary
218 Index
224 Picture Credits

Introduction

FRANK GEHRY: 'ARCHITECTURE SHOULD SPEAK OF ITS TIME AND PLACE,
BUT YEARN FOR TIMELESSNESS.'

First created as protection from the elements, architecture
has evolved throughout history to meet the diverse needs of
its many users. From the earliest dwellings to recent steel
and glass towers, the built environment has constantly
demonstrated human endeavour and achievement, with the
greatest architecture balancing form, function, structure
and aesthetics.

Buildings were first erected to provide shelter, but soon
more complex structures were built for religious rituals,
and these constitute some of the first surviving structures.
The earliest monumental buildings that we know of were
created by the ancient civilizations of Mesopotamia and
Egypt: brick-built ziggurats (temples) in Mesopotamia and
stone mastabas (tombs) in Egypt. Among other things, the
Mesopotamians pioneered urban planning and perceived
'the craft of building' as a divine gift bestowed by the gods.

Architecture continued to flourish, and in c.30–15 BCE,
the Roman architect and engineer Vitruvius wrote *De
Architectura*, which is considered to be the first book on
architectural theory and remained the main influence on
Western architects for over a thousand years.

Human needs continue to inspire some of the most
innovative architectural solutions, and this book explores
many of the remarkable ideas that have materialized over the
last 4,000 years. With a unique cross-referencing system, it
charts the history of architecture and investigates some of
the most significant works, styles, materials and elements of
architecture across the world.

Styles

FRANK LLOYD WRIGHT: 'THE MOTHER ART IS ARCHITECTURE.
WITHOUT AN ARCHITECTURE OF OUR OWN WE HAVE NO SOUL
OF OUR OWN CIVILIZATION.'

During certain time periods, particular styles of
architecture evolve, characterized by identifiable features
and shaped by a range of factors, including technology,
materials and the imagination of architects. As cultures

change, they merge or learn from each other, as in the case
of the ancient Greek and Roman civilizations, or conversely
they deliberately contradict previous ideas, for instance the
Postmodernist reaction against Modernism. Some styles use
completely new approaches and methods, while others, such
as Neoclassicism and the Gothic Revival, revisit previous
styles. Every revival, however, differs from the original,
reflecting the needs and technologies of its own period.
Some styles only develop in certain locations, such as
Khmer architecture or the Chicago School. Many evolve in
the wake of key architectural innovations, and some emerge
from travel and consequent cultural interchange, such as
Moorish architecture. Some styles are named long after
they occurred, such as the Renaissance; some are named as
they are created, such as Brutalism. Overall, even though
they often overlap, these styles help to clarify the history of
architecture. This section of the book explores many of the
most important styles as chronologically as possible.

The Buildings

ALVAR AALTO: 'THE ULTIMATE GOAL OF THE ARCHITECT …
IS TO CREATE A PARADISE. EVERY HOUSE, EVERY PRODUCT OF
ARCHITECTURE … SHOULD BE A FRUIT OF OUR ENDEAVOUR TO
BUILD AN EARTHLY PARADISE FOR PEOPLE.'

Evolving out of the human need for shelter and security,
of the desire to worship and of available resources and skills,
architecture is a cross between an art and a science.
As various cultures developed, knowledge and practices
were gained, and traditions founded, disseminated and built
upon, and architecture was established. In this section of the
book, 50 of the most significant works of architecture across
time and place are featured, including some of the most
respected and many that introduced key ideas, materials,
forms or technologies for the first time. The earliest architects
achieved results through trial and error, and as time passed,
theories and practicalities, failures and successes informed
subsequent architects, and architecture developed in diverse
and enterprising ways. Each work featured in this section
explores an important building or structure in architecture's
history that often incorporated cutting-edge materials and
methods, while consideration is also given to architects'
skills, aims and innovations.

Elements

ZAHA HADID: 'I DON'T THINK THAT ARCHITECTURE IS ONLY ABOUT SHELTER, IS ONLY ABOUT A VERY SIMPLE ENCLOSURE. IT SHOULD BE ABLE TO EXCITE YOU, TO CALM YOU, TO MAKE YOU THINK.'

Fundamental to architecture are the elements, or component parts. These include such things as balconies, arches, towers, staircases, arcades, courtyards and columns. Some elements are unusual, or only used in certain types of building, such as naves or minarets, while others are almost universal, for instance doors and windows. All are subject to considerations such as fashion, local preferences, accessible materials, religious specifications, climatic conditions, current regulations and technologies, plus the individual ideas of their architect. Some elements are similar, but with different interpretations, for instance the domes of Santa Maria del Fiore in Florence, Saint Basil's in Moscow and the Taj Mahal in Agra, or the spires of Cologne Cathedral, the Chrysler Building in New York City and the Sagrada Família in Barcelona. These illustrate how every architectural element is a complex combination of design, origins, influences, inventions and practicalities.

Materials

LUDWIG MIES VAN DER ROHE: 'ARCHITECTURE BEGINS WHEN YOU PLACE TWO BRICKS CAREFULLY TOGETHER.'

From mud to marble, brick to bamboo, stone to steel and concrete to carbon fibre, materials used in architecture have become broader as human requirements change and technology and engineering have progressed. Architectural possibilities that are enabled by using various materials are explained in this section, including both essential components such as stone or wood, and those that are predominantly used in parts of buildings and structures, such as glass and tiles. Some materials have been used continually for thousands of years, some are no longer used and others have been invented recently. Examples of where and how these materials have been used are explored in this section, while useful cross-references give further examples.

How to use this book

The book is divided into four areas – Styles, The Buildings, Elements and Materials – that explain key areas of architecture. Each is organized chronologically, but can be read in any order. Cross-references can be found at the foot of each page, giving helpful connections with other sections, while feature boxes discuss crucial developments and the backgrounds of the architects.

Key architects

Key developments

Cross-references to styles and materials

Architect and location

Building date

Background information on the architect and architecture

Major related works

Cross-references to styles, elements and materials

STYLES

ANCIENT EGYPTIAN 12 • PRE-COLUMBIAN 13 • ANCIENT GREEK 14 • BUDDHIST 15 ANCIENT ROMAN 16 • BYZANTINE 17 • JAPANESE 18 • HINDU 19 • ISLAMIC 20 KALINGA 21 • MOORISH 22 • KHMER 23 • ROMANESQUE 24 • GOTHIC 25 • RENAISS- ANCE 26 • MUGHAL 27 • PALLADIAN 28 • BAROQUE 29 • ROCOCO 30 • NEOCLASSICAL 31 • GOTHIC REVIVAL 32 • SHAKER 33 • CHICAGO SCHOOL 34 • ARTS AND CRAFTS 35 ART NOUVEAU 36 • MODERNIST 37 • ORGANIC 38 • FUTURIST 39 • EXPRESSIONIST 40 DE STIJL 41 • INTERNATIONAL STYLE 42 • BAUHAUS 43 • ART DECO 44 • GEODESIC 45 BRUTALIST 46 • POSTMODERN 47 • MINIMALIST 48 • HIGH-TECH 49 • SUSTAINABLE 50 DECONSTRUCTIVIST 51

Ancient Egyptian

2670 BCE – 336 CE

KEY ARCHITECTS: IMHOTEP • HEMIUNU • INENI • SENENMUT
AMENHOTEP, SON OF HAPU

Whether it was built for the dead or the living, ancient Egyptian architecture placed a strong emphasis on harmony with the surrounding landscape.

During the Old and Middle Kingdoms (c.2600–1800 BCE), pyramids were built as tombs for the pharaohs. The most imposing was the Great Pyramid at Giza, made for the Pharaoh Khufu in c.2589–2566 BCE. The pyramid's shape reached up to the gods, creating a commanding presence across the land. These huge constructions were built with meticulous precision, their massive stones so finely jointed that the edge of a knife cannot fit between them. The blocks were held together by mortar, and the entire structures were encased in white limestone, with their summits topped in gold. Within the pyramids, narrow passages led to the royal burial chambers.

Egyptian temples evolved from small shrines to large complexes, and by the New Kingdom (c.1550–1070 BCE) they had become massive stone structures consisting of halls and courtyards. Examples include the two massive Abu Simbel rock temples, which were carved out of the mountainside in the thirteenth century BCE as monuments for Ramesses II (c.1303–1213 BCE) and his queen Nefertari (d.1255 BCE). The main temple is famous for its four gigantic seated statues of Ramesses II, along with smaller statues of Nefertari and of his mother and children.

KEY DEVELOPMENTS
The earliest monumental works of architecture in ancient Egypt were made of mud-bricks, earth and wood, but later structures were built of stone, which became the dominant building material by c.2670 BCE. Alongside tombs and temples, forts and castles were constructed as massive strongholds, yet retaining the elegance and symmetry of the religious buildings.

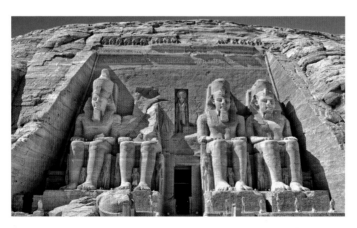

Abu Simbel Temple, architect unknown, c.1264 BCE, Aswan Governorate, Nubia, Egypt

GREAT PYRAMID **p.54** STAIRCASE **p.176** COLUMN **p.177** PORTICO/PORCH **p.186** STONE **p.192** MUD-BRICK/ADOBE **p.193** BRICK **p.195** PLASTER **p.203**

Pre-Columbian

KEY ARCHITECTS: NONE KNOWN

2000 BCE
–
1519 CE

Palace of Palenque,
architect unknown,
7th–8th centuries
CE, Chiapas, Mexico

For over 3,000 years before the Europeans 'discovered' America, complex societies had already been established across North, Central and South America.

Well before the Spanish conquest in the sixteenth century, Pre-Columbian Mesoamerican architecture had been created by numerous civilizations for a wide variety of purposes. Although knowledge of astronomy and engineering was limited, structures and buildings were often aligned with astronomical features or with the cardinal directions. Much of the architecture developed through cultural exchange – for instance the Aztecs learnt much from earlier Mayan architecture.

Many cultures built entire cities, including monolithic temples and pyramids decoratively carved with animals, gods and kings. The arrangements of these cities seem to have mythological and symbolic meanings. Most had a central plaza with government buildings and temples, plus public ball courts, or *tlachtli*, on raised platforms. Pyramids were a dominating feature, generally stepped. They were probably not used as burial chambers, but had important religious sites at the top. Many of the best-known are in Mexico, including the Pyramid of the Sun and Pyramid of the Moon (both c.200–50 CE) at Teotihuacan, the Castillo (c.600–1000 CE) at Chichen Itza, and largest of all, the Great Pyramid (c.300 BCE –c.900 CE) at Cholula.

KEY DEVELOPMENTS
A complex of connected buildings and courtyards, the Palace of Palenque was built over several generations as both a royal residence and an administrative centre. It comprised twelve houses, two courts and a square tower on four levels that dominated the site. A small stream at the back was channelled into a vaulted aqueduct.

TEMPLE OF INSCRIPTIONS **p.64** ROOF **p.168** ARCH **p.173** TOWER **p.174** STAIRCASE **p.176** STONE **p.192** MUD-BRICK/ADOBE **p.193** STUCCO **p.205**

Ancient Greek

850 BCE – 600 CE

KEY ARCHITECTS: ICTINUS • CALLIKRATES • KARPION • PARMENION
PHAEAX • PHIDIAS • AELIUS NICON • LIBON • SATYROS

KEY DEVELOPMENTS
Commonly considered the 'father' of urban planning, Hippodamus of Miletus (498–408 BCE) planned cities in grid systems, with parallel streets, central public spaces, and functions and activities grouped together. Ancient Greek architects used the orders in a wide range of building types, including public, sacred and private.

Temple of Hephaestus, architect unknown, c.449 BCE, Agoraios Kolonos Hill, Athens, Greece

From approximately c.850 BCE to 600 CE, ancient Greek culture flourished on the Greek mainland, on the Peloponnese, and on the Aegean islands.

By the fourth century BCE, its architects and stonemasons had developed a system of rules for all building known as the orders. These are most easily recognized in three types of column. The Doric column is relatively stout and plain; the Ionic is slimmer with four scroll-like curls at the corners of its capital; and the most ornate is the Corinthian, often decorated with carved acanthus leaves and four scrolls, or with lotus or palm leaves.

Overall, the architecture appeared plain, but sculptural decorations were elaborate, appearing on column capitals and pediments, in friezes, metopes and triglyphs, and as statues. All were painted in bright colours.

The most important buildings were temples and theatres, which used a complex mix of optical illusions and balanced ratios. From c.550 to 404 BCE, the Acropolis was built on a rocky hill in Athens – the buildings there represent the pinnacle of Greek architectural achievement, and include the Parthenon, the Propylaea, the Erechtheion and the Temple of Athena Nike. Completed in 432 BCE, the Parthenon follows the Doric ratio of 9:4, but also has Ionic features. Unlike most Greek temples, which have six marble supporting columns across the front, the Parthenon has eight. In total, it has 47 columns, each over 10 metres (30 feet) high and with a slight parabolic upward curve to shed water and reinforce against earthquakes.

PARTHENON **p.56** ROOF **p.168** COLUMN **p.177** PORTICO/PORCH **p.186** STONE **p.192** MARBLE **p.200**

Buddhist

507 BCE
–

KEY ARCHITECTS: NONE KNOWN

Buddhist architecture developed in the Indian subcontinent during the fourth to the second century BCE, and spread first to China and then further across Asia.

Indian emperor Ashoka (r. c.265–c.236 BCE) saw Buddhism as a way of uniting his vast region, and so had stupas constructed throughout the land. A stupa (Sanskrit for heap) is a domed structure containing relics, used as a place of meditation to commemorate the Buddha. The dome symbolized the infinite space of the sky. Stupas became places of pilgrimage, achieving what Ashoka intended: the spread of Buddhism. Monasteries, or viharas, were built near to stupas and also at the sites of major events in the Buddha's life.

The earliest surviving stupas are at Sanchi, surrounded by elaborate stone archways placed at the four cardinal points. The most monumental Buddhist stupa that remains is at Borobudur, Java (9th century CE). It consists of a central stupa at the top of nine terraces containing many smaller stupas. As Buddhism spread to places including Nepal, Tibet, Japan, Sri Lanka, Thailand, Korea, China and Myanmar, the architecture retained some features of the earliest Indian examples but also acquired various local characteristics – the pagoda is just one evolution of the Indian stupa.

KEY DEVELOPMENTS
Three types of structure are associated with Buddhist architecture: stupas, viharas, and *chaityas* or *chaitya-grihas* (shrines or prayer halls, later called temples). Among the most important Buddhist temples are Haeinsa (Temple of Reflection on a Smooth Sea) in Gyeongsang, South Korea; Wat Arun (Temple of Dawn) in Bangkok, Thailand; and the Jokhang Temple in Tibet.

Sanchi Stupa, architect unknown, 3rd century BCE–c.100 BCE, Madhya Pradesh, India

SANCHI STUPA **p.58** ROOF **p.168** DOME **p.172** ARCH **p.173** COLUMN **p.177** SPIRE **p.184** STONE **p.192** BRICK **p.195** WOOD **p.196**

Ancient Roman

484 BCE
–
608 CE

KEY ARCHITECTS: HERMODORUS OF SALAMIS • RABIRIUS
POLLODORUS OF DAMASCUS • VITRUVIUS • SEVERUS • DECRIANUS

Pont du Gard, architect unknown, 1st century CE, Vers-Pont-du-Gard, France

Wherever the Roman army conquered, they established towns and cities, spreading their empire and advancing their architectural and engineering achievements.

Surpassing most civilizations of their time, the Romans built a vast empire, developing engineering skills, architectural techniques and new materials. They built increasingly ambitious temples, aqueducts, amphitheatres, triumphal arches and more. Using free-standing columns, they developed the rounded stone arch, and from this developed arcades and aqueducts, in which water was carried through cement-lined channels. They also developed the cross vault and the dome. Between 30 and 15 BCE, the architect and civil and military engineer Marcus Vitruvius Pollio published a major treatise, *De Architectura,* which influenced architects around the world for centuries.

Between 72 and 80 CE, an amphitheatre was built in Rome of concrete, limestone and tuff (volcanic ash). The largest amphitheatre ever built, the elliptical Colosseum could hold around 50,000 spectators. Another great achievement demonstrating Roman precision was the Pont du Gard in southern France, the highest surviving ancient Roman aqueduct. In the first century CE, a long, winding aqueduct was built underground to carry water from a spring to the Roman colony of Nîmes, but it emerged to cross over the Gardon River via this huge, three-tiered arched bridge.

KEY DEVELOPMENTS
Among the many Roman architectural achievements were domes, which were created for temples, baths, villas, palaces and tombs, with thickened walls to provide support. One example, the Pantheon in Rome, was commissioned by the Emperor Trajan in c.114 CE as part of the Baths of Agrippa. It is the largest surviving Roman dome and has a large oculus at its centre.

PANTHEON **p.60** DOME **p.172** ARCH **p.173** COLUMN **p.177** STONE **p.192** BRICK **p.195** WOOD **p.196** TILES **p.198** CONCRETE **p.201**

Byzantine

330
—
1453 CE

KEY ARCHITECTS: ANTHEMIUS • ISIDORE • TRDAT • CALLINICUS • RUFINUS
PETRONAS KAMATEROS • PERALTA • ASTRAS

In 330 CE, Emperor Constantine transferred the imperial capital of Rome to Byzantium and named it Constantinople (now called Istanbul).

Constantinople was an important part of many trade routes. Byzantine architects fused Roman elements with eastern influences, and these architectural ideas spread and evolved, appearing in parts of Italy, Syria, Greece, Russia and Asia Minor, mainly in churches with domed roofs, arches and spires.

Among its most distinctive elements are domes attached to square bases through one of two methods. One is the squinch, an arch in each corner of the base that crosses diagonally under the dome. The other is the pendentive, invented by the Byzantines, in which a curved, triangular section of vaulting is erected in each corner. Byzantine architecture often featured marble columns, coffered ceilings and sumptuous decoration, including the extensive use of mosaics. Later, the Greek cruciform plan (a cross with four equal arms) became an important part of Byzantine churches.

Over the years, Byzantine architecture became more complex, using fired bricks and plaster, as well as thin sheets of alabaster for windows. It lasted until Constantinople fell to the Turks in 1453, but continued to influence European builders for centuries.

KEY DEVELOPMENTS
Commissioned by Emperor Justinian, Hagia Sophia influenced Byzantine architecture profoundly. Following its example, large central domes were often surrounded by lower, smaller domes in religious buildings such as San Vitale (527–47 CE) in Ravenna (see page 204), Saint Mark's (1093) in Venice and Saint Basil's (1555–61) in Moscow.

Hagia Sophia,
Isidore and
Anthemius,
532–7 CE,
Istanbul, Turkey

HAGIA SOPHIA **p.62** ARCADE **p.171** DOME **p.172** ARCH **p.173** COLUMN **p.177** SPIRE **p.184**
STONE **p.192** BRICK **p.195** WOOD **p.196** MARBLE **p.200** MOSAIC **p.204**

Japanese

538 CE

KEY ARCHITECTS: TAKEDA AYASABURO • ARATA ENDO • TATSUNO KINGO
SONE TATSUZO • KENZO TANGE • FUMIHIKO MAKI

Traditionally, Japanese architecture was made of wood with *fusuma* (sliding doors) in place of walls, allowing internal spaces to be altered to suit different purposes.

Early Japanese buildings include the Shinto Ise shrines (third century CE on), which were made of cypress wood and resemble granaries. The introduction of Buddhism in the sixth century initiated large-scale wooden temple building with an emphasis on simplicity, and much of the architecture was imported from China and other Asian cultures.

In contrast with Western architecture, these structures rarely use stone, except for specific elements such as foundations. Wooden posts and lintels support large, gently curving roofs with eaves that extend over verandas. Walls are light, thin, never load-bearing and often movable. Early temples resembled those in China, with wide courtyards and symmetrical plans.

During the Azuchi-Momoyama period (1568–1600), many castles were built. Most had a central tower or *tenshu* (heaven defence) surrounded by gardens and fortified buildings, all within massive stone walls and surrounded by moats. Interiors had spaces separated by sliding *fusuma* as well as *byobu* (folding screens).

The late nineteenth century saw the adoption of traditional Western styles, but the influence of modernism was felt from the 1920s. A radical architectural movement developed in the 1960s called Metabolism, or the Burnt Ash School. Its advocates designed megastructural projects that promoted renewal and regeneration.

KEY DEVELOPMENTS
Built from the early 7th century CE as the private temple of Crown Prince Shotoku (574–622 CE), Horyu-ji consists of 41 independent buildings including the main worship hall, or *kon-do* (golden hall) and the five-storey pagoda set in the centre of an open area surrounded by a roofed cloister, or *kairo*. The *kon-do* is topped by a ceramic-tiled irimoya roof.

Horyu-ji, architect unknown, 607–710 CE, Ikaruga, Nara Prefecture, Japan

RINSHUNKAKU **p.100** DOOR **p.166** TOWER **p.174** COLUMN **p.177** PORTICO/PORCH **p.186** WOOD **p.196** PAPER **p.197** CONCRETE **p.201**

Hindu

KEY ARCHITECTS: NONE KNOWN

C.500
—
1910 CE

Across the Indian subcontinent, Hindu architecture evolved from simple rock-cut cave shrines to monumental temples.

From the fourth to fifth centuries CE, Hindu temples were adapted to the worship of different deities and regional beliefs, and by the sixth or seventh centuries had evolved into towering brick- or stone-built structures that symbolized the sacred five-peaked Mount Meru. Influenced by early Buddhist stupas, the architecture was not designed for collective worship, but had areas for worshippers to leave offerings and perform rituals. Hindu culture encouraged creative independence, but architects had to adhere to certain 'rules', including precise, harmonious geometry throughout, tall towers and sculptures of gods, worshippers, erotic scenes and animals, along with floral and geometric patterns.

Most Hindu temples were built on an *adhisthana* (carved platform), and each includes an inner sanctum, the *garbhagriha* (womb-chamber), where the image of the primary deity is housed. Above the *garbhagriha* is the tower-like *shikhara* (also known as *vimana*) and walkways devoted to *parikrama* (circumambulation). Also featured is a congregation hall, and some-times an antechamber and an *ardhaman-dapa*, or portico entrance. Every temple is surrounded by walls containing huge, ornate gateways called *gopurams* facing in each of the cardinal directions.

KEY DEVELOPMENTS
Built in the 19th century with the traditional nine spires of Bengal architecture, the three-storeyed Dakshineswar Kali Temple stands on an *adhisthana* with a columned veranda. The *garbhagriha* houses an idol of the goddess Kali, and the entire temple compound contains a large courtyard, with rooms along the boundary walls and 12 shrines dedicated to Shiva.

Dakshineswar Kali Temple, architect unknown, 1855, Kolkata, India

PRAMBANAN **p.70** DOME **p.172** TOWER **p.174** STONE **p.192** BRICK **p.195**

Islamic

KEY ARCHITECTS: MIMAR SINAN • SEDEFKAR MEHMED AGHA
USTAD ISA SHIRAZI • ATIK SINAN

KEY DEVELOPMENTS
During the Abbasid dynasty (750–1258 CE), the Islamic capital moved from Damascus to Baghdad and then from Baghdad to Samarra. The huge, rectangular Great Mosque of al-Mutawakkil at Samarra was built between 848 and 851 CE, and combines hypostyle architecture (a roof supported by columns) with a huge spiralling minaret, known as the *malwiya* (snail-shell) minaret.

Great Mosque of al-Mutawakkil, architect unknown, 848–51 CE, Samarra, Iraq

After the death in 632 CE of the founder of Islam, the Prophet Muhammad, the Islamic empire grew rapidly.

By 750 CE, it stretched from Spain and Morocco in the west, to central Asia and Afghanistan in the east. Comprising mainly mosques, tombs, palaces and forts, Islamic architecture drew on influences from Persian, Roman, Byzantine, Chinese and Indian architecture, but developed its own unique aspects. Significant features include repeated patterns, calligraphy, precise geometry, domes, arches and minarets.

Domes first appeared in 691 CE with the construction of the Dome of the Rock (Qubbat al-Sakhrah) in Jerusalem, based on the nearby Church of the Holy Sepulchre (335 CE). Most common are drum domes, but also distinctive are pointed domes, as at the Taj Mahal (see page 98). Arches are another notable element, for instance the horseshoe or Moorish arch, the semi-circular or Roman arch, and scalloped trefoil, quatrefoil, cinquefoil or multifoil arches, which are specific to the Moorish architecture (see page 22) and were often used to create colonnades. After the Ottomans captured Constantinople in 1453, they converted the Hagia Sophia (see page 62) into a mosque, which then served as a model for many other Ottoman mosques such as the Süleymaniye Mosque (1558) in Istanbul.

DOME OF THE ROCK **p.68** GREAT MOSQUE OF DJENNÉ **p.126** DOME **p.172** ARCH **p.173** TOWER **p.174**
COLUMN **p.177** STONE **p.192** BRICK **p.195**

Kalinga

KEY ARCHITECTS: NONE KNOWN

c.650
—
c.1550 CE

Lingaraja Temple, architect unknown, c.1060, Bhubaneswar, Odisha, India

The ancient Kalinga region corresponds to the present-day eastern Indian areas of Odisha, West Bengal and northern Andhra Pradesh.

Its architecture reached a peak between the ninth and twelfth centuries under the patronage of the Somavamsi dynasty of Odisha. Lavishly sculpted with hundreds of figures, Kalinga temples usually feature repeating forms such as horseshoes. Within the protective walls of the temple complex are three main buildings with distinctive curved towers called *deul* or *deula* and prayer halls called *jagmohan*. The *rekha deula* is the sanctuary, topped by a tall curving, pointed tower; the *pidha deula* are square halls with pyramid-shaped roofs;

and the *khakhara deula* is a rectangular building, also with a pyramid-shaped roof, usually shorter than the *rekha deula* but taller than the *pidha deula*. It provides one of the main areas for prayer and offerings. *Khakhara* derives from the word *khakharu*, meaning pumpkin or gourd, reflecting the building's gourd-like shape.

KEY DEVELOPMENTS

One of the oldest temples in Bhubaneswar, the capital of the state of Odisha, the Lingaraja Temple faces east and is built of sandstone and laterite. Within its thick surrounding walls are 150 smaller shrines. The main tower or *deul* is 45 m (148 ft) high and extravagantly sculpted with a profusion of figures and other religious motifs.

 TEMPLE OF THE SUN **p.88** TOWER **p.174** SPIRE **p.184** STONE **p.192** MUD-BRICK/ADOBE **p.193** BRICK **p.195** GLASS **p.206**

Moorish

KEY ARCHITECTS: NONE KNOWN

711
–
1492 CE

KEY DEVELOPMENTS
As well as mosques, palaces and fortifications, the Moors built elaborate courtyards and gardens, with fountains, colonnades and cloisters. Architects worked with craft workers who designed patterned tiles called *zellij* in Arabic and *azulejo* in Spanish and Portuguese. These decorative tiles were integrated into the architecture and used in both religious and secular buildings.

The Great Mosque, architect unknown, 784–987 CE, Cordoba, Spain

From approximately 711 to 1492, Arabs conquered and dominated large parts of southern Europe and North Africa.

Europeans called the new settlers Moors, and their secular and religious architecture came to dominate these regions. It featured distinct Islamic elements as well as others taken from these new surroundings, adapted and developed for such buildings as the Alhambra palace and the Generalife (1302–19) in Granada, and the Great Mosque at Cordoba, built from 784 to 987 CE in four phases. The Great Mosque features elaborate internal decorations and includes an immense prayer hall, with 850 columns and double arches in contrasting red- and cream-coloured stone.

Crenellated, ogee and lancet arches are common in Moorish architecture, but it is particularly noted for its dramatically curved horseshoe arches. Along with large domes and repeated decorative patterns, *muqarnas*, sometimes called honeycomb or stalactite vaults, were an Islamic feature that Moorish architects developed and adapted to great effect. These highly decorative vaults were used to adorn pendentives, alcoves, arches, domes and half-domes. Major buildings were often served by complex irrigation and plumbing systems developed by Moorish engineers.

ALHAMBRA **p.80** DOME **p.172** ARCH **p.173** COLUMN **p.177** STONE **p.192** BRICK **p.195** TILES **p.198** MARBLE **p.200** GLASS **p.206**

Khmer

825
–
C.1450 CE

KEY ARCHITECTS: NONE KNOWN

From the start of the ninth century to the early fifteenth century, Khmer kings ruled over a vast Hindu-Buddhist empire in Southeast Asia.

Angkor, in present-day Cambodia, was its capital city, and most of its surviving buildings are east-facing stone temples, many of them constructed in pyramidal, tiered forms consisting of five square structures with towers, or *prasats*, that represent the sacred five-peaked Mount Meru of Hindu, Jain and Buddhist doctrine. According to these religions, the gods live in the mountain at the centre of the universe, with different deities living on the different levels. As it was not intended as a place of worship but a home to a particular deity,

each sanctuary is only a few metres across, with its importance conveyed by the height and position of the *prasat*, the central one being dominant. A moat surrounding the temple symbolizes the cosmic ocean.

As the residences of gods, temples were made of durable materials such as sandstone, brick or laterite, a clay-like substance that dries hard. Mount Meru is believed to be guarded at the four cardinal points by celestial guardians, so Khmer temples feature embellished, monumental gatehouse towers called *gopuras* to the north, south, east and west.

KEY DEVELOPMENTS
Temples were intricately carved with religious images and important events of Khmer history, although Buddhist temples are generally less ornate than Hindu equivalents. Within their cities, Khmer architects also built vast reservoirs that collected heavy rainfall each monsoon season and water from nearby rivers to serve the population.

Ta Prohm Temple, architect unknown, 1186, Angkor, Siem Reap Province, Cambodia

ANGKOR WAT **p.74** ROOF **p.168** TOWER **p.174** COLUMN **p.177** STONE **p.192** BRICK **p.195** TILES **p.198**

Romanesque

1000
–
1150

KEY ARCHITECTS: MASTER MATEO • BENEDETTO ANTELAMI • LANFRANCO
DIOTISALVI

KEY DEVELOPMENTS
One of the finest examples of
High Romanesque architecture
is the Benedictine Maria
Laach Abbey in the Rhineland,
Germany. It has six heavy
towers, two circular and four
square, while other features
include a cloistered atrium,
square piers, arched and round
windows and rich carvings on
the column capitals.

Maria Laach Abbey, architect unknown,
1093–1230, Rhineland-Palatinate,
Germany

A large number of heavy stone churches
with rounded arches, barrel or groin vaulting and huge piers were built in Europe
between approximately 1000 and 1150.

By the nineteenth century, the term
Romanesque was used to describe this
architecture, with its angular towers,
large naves and carved, rounded arches.
Borrowing from ancient Roman styles and
methods, the Romanesque style was also
influenced by Carolingian, Byzantine and
Islamic architecture. Although the evolution of the style is not precisely defined,
it was the first since the Roman empire to
develop across Europe.

Romanesque architecture reached
maturity in c.1000, when new churches
were constructed along pilgrimage
routes in Spain and France. These had
to have large enough capacities to house
many pilgrims at once. To achieve this,
architects reintroduced vaulting from
Roman precedents, creating wide, high
ceilings. They also built radiating chapels
around the sides of church interiors for
private worship. Elaborate stone carving
was revived and developed, with stone
reliefs and sculpture adorning interior and
exterior walls that depicted biblical narra-
tives. Many national variations developed,
included the perpendicular arches of the
German Romanesque and twin towers
in Normandy.

MARIA LAACH ABBEY **p.72** ROOF **p.168** ARCH **p.173** TOWER **p.174** ATRIUM **p.180** NAVE **p.182**
STONE **p.192** BRICK **p.195** TILES **p.198** GLASS **p.206**

Gothic

1140 – 1525

KEY ARCHITECTS: MATEUS FERNANDES • ARNOLFO DI CAMBIO
MATTHIAS OF ARRAS • JEAN DE CHELLES • HEINRICH PARLER • CONRAD PFLÜGER

KEY DEVELOPMENTS
Until the 16th century, Gothic architecture was called *Opus Francigenum* (French work). Its earlier phases are often categorized as Early Gothic (1140–1250) and High Gothic (c.1250–1300) before national variants emerged, such as the English Perpendicular style and the French and Spanish Flamboyant styles, all of which featured greater embellishments, especially highly elaborate window tracery.

Chartres Cathedral, architect unknown, 1194–1250, Chartres, France

The Gothic style began in 1140 when Abbot Suger (c.1081–1151) had a new choir constructed for the abbey of Saint-Denis.

Suger wrote of the light that was to pervade his new church and create a sense of awe among worshippers. To this end, he commissioned pointed arches, cross-rib vaulting and huge stained-glass windows, which came to define the new architecture.

Flying buttresses were among the great engineering achievements of the Gothic style. These great arched structures on buildings' exteriors supported and distributed the weight of the high vaulted ceilings. The jewel-coloured windows meant that churches were flooded with light and colour, and the combination of elements influenced church-building for more than three centuries. The first Gothic cathedral, Chartres, is built on a cruciform plan and dominated by two contrasting spires, its flying buttresses and a façade carved with biblical stories.

Tall, pointed spires were also used on a grand scale in Gothic churches, and had the double role of being visible from great distances to reassure and guide the faithful, while also conveying a powerful impression of pointing directly up to God. Inside, as well as the colours from stained-glass windows, pillars rose to lofty heights above worshippers, carrying arching vaults high above. The effect of such Gothic churches was to represent heaven on earth.

CHARTRES CATHEDRAL **p.78** DOGE'S PALACE **p.86** ARCH **p.173** TOWER **p.174** SPIRE **p.184**
BUTTRESS **p.178** NAVE **p.182** VAULT **p.183** STONE **p.192** BRICK **p.195** STAINED GLASS **p.207**

Renaissance

C.1452
–
1580

KEY ARCHITECTS: FILIPPO BRUNELLESCHI • LEON BATTISTA ALBERTI
ANDREA PALLADIO • DONATO BRAMANTE • MICHELANGELO BUONARROTI

KEY DEVELOPMENTS

Donato Bramante created a new style of church incorporating elements of ancient temples. They were centrally planned, based on squares, circles and octagons. His circular Tempietto in Rome is a small shrine that blends classical antique elements with new ideas. The dome, colonnade and entablature derive from Roman styles, but the balustrade and symbols of Christianity are new.

Tempietto di San Pietro, Donato
Bramante, 1502, Rome, Italy

During the Renaissance, Italy was a collection of city-states, and intense rivalry between them generated an increase in technical and artistic developments.

The period began in around 1452, when the architect and humanist Leon Battista Alberti (1404–72) completed his treatise *De Re Aedificatoria* (*On the Art of Building*) after studying the ancient ruins of Rome and Vitruvius's *De Architectura*. His writing covered numerous subjects, including history, town planning, engineering, sacred geometry, humanism and philosophies of beauty, and set out the key elements of architecture and its ideal proportions. Student architects increasingly visited Rome to study the ancient buildings and ruins, especially the Colosseum and Pantheon (see page 60). Soon, grand buildings were constructed in Florence using this new style, including the Pazzi Chapel (1441–78) and the Pitti Palace (1458–64).

An incredible feat of engineering, the massive dome of Florence's cathedral, Santa Maria del Fiore (1294–1436), was designed by Filippo Brunelleschi, whose discovery of linear perspective led to the development of detailed architectural drawings. The Santa Maria del Fiore was Pre-Renaissance, and introduced several Renaissance ideas. The Renaissance began in Italy, but slowly spread to other parts of Europe, with varying interpretations.

SANTA MARIA DEL FIORE **p.82** DOME **p.172** ARCH **p.173** TOWER **p.174** COLUMN **p.177** NAVE **p.182** STONE **p.192** BRICK **p.195** MARBLE **p.200** STAINED GLASS **p.207**

Mughal

1526 – 1857

KEY ARCHITECTS: MIRAK MIRZA GHIYAS • MIR ABDUL KARIM
MAKRAMAT KHAN • USTAD AHMAD LAHORI • USTAD ISA SHIRAZI

Lahore Fort, various architects,
1566–18th century, Lahore, Pakistan

KEY DEVELOPMENTS
The huge fort at the northern
end of Lahore's Walled City in
Pakistan was almost entirely
rebuilt in 1566 during Akbar's
reign. Later, detailed decorations were added, including
marble and inlaid designs,
mirrors and mosaics of highly
polished coloured stones
known as pietra dura. Its grand
Alamgiri Gate was constructed
under Emperor Aurangzeb, who
reigned from 1658 to 1707.

The Mughal period (1526–1857) witnessed
an evolution of architecture in northern
and central India that amalgamated Hindu
and Muslim elements drawn from both
India and Persia.

In the Mughal period, double domes,
recessed archways, symmetry and delicate
decoration were prominent. The style first
developed under Akbar the Great (1542–
1605) with the Tomb of Emperor Humayun
(1508–56) in Delhi. Commissioned in
1565 by Humayun's first wife, Empress
Bega Begum (c.1522–82), and designed by
Persian architect Mirak Mirza Ghiyas, it
was the first structure to use red sandstone
on a large scale, and the first Indian building to feature a Persian double dome.

Mughal architecture reached its peak
under Emperor Shah Jahan, who reigned
from 1628 to 1658, in particular with the
Taj Mahal in Agra, a white marble mausoleum commissioned in 1632. Standing
on a large square plinth, it has four
almost identical façades, each with a high
arch-shaped doorway, topped by a large
double dome and a finial that combines
Islamic and Hindu symbolism. Four tall
minarets extend from the plinth corners,
and the exterior decorations include
calligraphy, abstract forms, verses from the
Qu'ran and vegetable motifs, while interior
surfaces are inlaid with precious and
semi-precious gemstones.

TAJ MAHAL **p.98** DOME **p.172** ARCH **p.173** TOWER **p.174** BRICK **p.195** TILES **p.198**
MARBLE **p.200** GLASS **p.206**

Palladian

1556
–
1736

KEY ARCHITECTS: ANDREA PALLADIO • WILLIAM KENT • HENRY FLITCROFT
INIGO JONES • VINCENZO SCAMOZZI • COLEN CAMPBELL • RICHARD BOYLE

*Chiswick House,
Richard Boyle
(Lord Burlington)
and William
Kent, 1726–9,
Chiswick,
London, UK*

Named after the Italian Renaissance archi-tect Andrea Palladio, the style known as Palladian architecture remained popular in Europe and America from the seventeenth to the nineteenth centuries.

Focusing on the theories of Vitruvius, Palladio and his assistant Vincenzo Scamozzi re-interpreted Roman architec-ture. In 1570, Palladio published *I Quattro Libri dell'Architettura* (*The Four Books of Architecture*), explaining how he based his work on symmetry, proportion and a per-sonal interpretation of the classical orders.

Inigo Jones took Palladio's ideas to Britain, combining them with elements from other Renaissance architects. Two of his Palladian designs in London are the Banqueting House (1619–22) at Whitehall and the Queen's House (1616–35) in Greenwich. Expressed slightly differently in each country, Palladianism appeared in churches, palaces, country houses and civic buildings, with a particularly strong influence in domestic architecture. Porticos were a prominent element, and classical-looking façades were designed to give panoramic views. The balance of empty space and solid structure was emphasized, and Palladian villas were built on podiums approached by grand staircases.

In the United States, Palladianism remained the prevailing style for public buildings until the 1930s, and even today much architecture follows Palladio's ideas about planning and proportion.

KEY DEVELOPMENTS

Seemingly inspired by Palladio's 16th-century Villa La Rotonda, Chiswick House demonstrates the symmetrical emphasis of Palladianism with its portico and Corinthian columns at the front. Above, a shallow, stepped dome derived from the Pantheon tops an octagonal space and obelisks disguise chimney stacks. At the rear are three Serlian windows, also popularized by Palladio.

VILLA LA ROTONDA **p.96** DOME **p.172** STAIRCASE **p.176** COLUMN **p.177**
STONE **p.192** BRICK **p.195** MARBLE **p.200** CONCRETE **p.201** STUCCO **p.205** GLASS **p.206**

Baroque

1624 – 1746

KEY ARCHITECTS: GIAN LORENZO BERNINI • CARLO MADERNO • JOHANN BERNHARD FISCHER VON ERLACH • FRANCESCO BORROMINI

The first truly international architectural movement, Baroque spread throughout Europe and Latin America, with interpretations varying widely.

The Baroque emerged, belatedly, out of the Counter Reformation as an attempt by the Catholic Church in Rome to convey its power and to emphasize the magnificence of God. Describing an oddly shaped pearl, the Portuguese word *barroco* was adopted for this extravagant, dramatic and irregular art and design style, which lasted from the early seventeenth century until the mid-eighteenth century.

The first Baroque buildings were cathedrals, churches and monasteries, soon joined by civic buildings, mansions and palaces. Characterized by complexity and dynamism, for the first time walls, façades and interiors curved and undulated, twists and spirals appeared, and contrasts of light and shadow were emphasized. Vaulted and ornately painted trompe-l'œil ceilings were common. Among several other innovations, Gian Lorenzo Bernini (1598–1680) introduced spiral columns in his great baldacchino of 1623 in Saint Peter's, Rome. One of his rivals, Francesco Borromini (1599–1667) created distinctive, quirky designs, using symbolism and manipulating classical forms, while another, Pietro Cortona (1596–1669), created one of the first curved façades for his church of Santi Luca e Martina (1635–64) in Rome.

KEY DEVELOPMENTS
Conveying drama, balance and stability, Santa Maria della Salute is one of the earliest Baroque churches in Venice. Designed by Baldassare Longhena (1598–1682), it is a vast, octagonal building, built on a wooden platform, with two domes and two tapering campanili (bell towers). Huge scroll-like volutes act as buttresses to the drum of the main dome.

Santa Maria della Salute, Baldassare Longhena, 1631–87, Venice, Italy

SAINT PETER'S BASILICA **p.90**   PALACE OF VERSAILLES **p.102**   DOME **p.172**   ARCH **p.173**   TOWER **p.174** COLUMN **p.177**   VAULT **p.183**   STONE **p.192**   BRICK **p.195**   MARBLE **p.200**   GLASS **p.206**

Rococo

1717
–
1766

KEY ARCHITECTS: FRANCESCO BARTOLOMEO RASTRELLI • MATEUS VICENTE
DE OLIVEIRA • JOHANN MICHAEL FISCHER • JUSTE-AURÈLE MEISSONNIER

In contrast to the heavy grandeur of the Baroque exterior of the Palace of Versailles, its Rococo interiors were lighter and more frivolous and exuberant.

The name Rococo derives from the French words *rocaille*, which describes shell-covered rock-work, and *coquille*, meaning seashell. Rococo architecture is fancy and fluid, accentuating asymmetry, with an abundant use of curves, scrolls, gilding and ornament. Whimsical and extravagant, the style enjoyed great popularity with the ruling elite of Europe during the eighteenth century, but it was to prove fairly short-lived.

Rococo architecture developed in France out of a new fashion in interior decoration, and spread across Europe. It often includes delicate ornamentation, gold and soft colours, and sometimes displays a Chinese influence. One of the most famous Rococo works of architecture is the Wieskirche in Steingaden, Germany, built from 1745 to 1754. The brothers Dominikus and Johann Baptist Zimmermann designed it as an oval building, with columns, cornices and wooden vaulting, and filled it with elaborate, gilded stucco and colourful trompe-l'œil paintings.

Other important Rococo buildings include the Queluz National Palace (1747–92) in Portugal, designed by Mateus Vicente de Oliveira (1706–86), and the trefoil-shaped Chinese House (1754–64) in Potsdam, Germany, by Johann Gottfried Büring (1723–after 1788) with gilded external pillars and Chinoiserie.

KEY DEVELOPMENTS
Conveying the absolute power of the monarchy, the Catherine Palace is as vast and resplendent as the Winter Palace (1754) in Saint Petersburg and the Palace of Versailles. Built for the Empress Elizabeth (1709–62) and named after her mother, the flamboyant stucco façade is broken up by regular pedimented bays, gilded with gold and featuring elaborate balconies.

Catherine Palace, Francesco Bartolomeo Rastrelli, 1752–6, Tsarskoye Selo, Russia

PALACE OF VERSAILLES **p.102** WIESKIRCHE **p.108** DOME **p.172** TOWER **p.174** VAULT **p.183** COURTYARD **p.175** COLUMN **p.177** STONE **p.192** BRICK **p.195** MARBLE **p.200** STUCCO **p.205** GLASS **p.206**

Neoclassical

1748 – 1850

KEY ARCHITECTS: JACQUES-GERMAIN SOUFFLOT • JOHN SOANE • JOHN NASH
CARL GOTTHARD LANGHANS • ROBERT ADAM • GIACOMO QUARENGHI

Neoclassical architecture focused on Greek or Roman details, plain, white walls and grandeur of scale.

Excavations during the eighteenth century at Pompeii and Herculaneum, which had both been buried beneath volcanic ash during the 79 CE eruption of Mount Vesuvius, inspired a return to order and rationality. One of the first Neoclassical buildings, the Church of Saint Geneviève, Paris (1756–97), was designed by Jacques Germain Soufflot (1713–80), but became a secular mausoleum, the Panthéon, in 1791. At the same time, Claude-Nicolas Ledoux (1736–1806) explored pure form through his buildings and town planning. In Berlin, Karl Friedrich Schinkel (1781–1841) based his Altes Museum (1823–30) on the Pantheon in Rome, while Carl Gotthard

Langhans (1732–1808) designed the Brandenburg Gate (1793) inspired by the Propylaea in Athens. In Britain, John Nash (1752–1835) and John Wood the Younger (1728–81) reshaped London and Bath with Neoclassical streets, crescents and parks, while in Russia Charles Cameron (1745–1812) designed the Pavlovsk Palace in Saint Petersburg (1782–6).

The style became extremely popular in newly independent America, adopted in Washington, DC, for the Capitol Building by William Thornton and Thomas Ustick Walter, and for the White House (1792–1829; see page 177) by James Hoban (1758–1831). The style's clean lines and sense of balance and proportion worked well for grand buildings and for smaller structures alike.

KEY DEVELOPMENTS
The third president of the United States, Thomas Jefferson, drew upon Palladian and classical ideals in his designs for the Virginia State Capitol, Richmond (1788) and the Rotunda at the University of Virginia, Charlottesville (1822–6). He based the proportions of the Rotunda directly on the Pantheon, and also followed Palladio's principles.

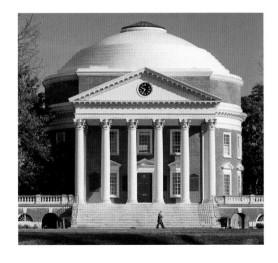

The Rotunda, Thomas Jefferson, 1822–6, Charlottesville, Virginia, USA

CAPITOL BUILDING **p.112** DOME **p.172** ARCH **p.173** COLUMN **p.177** VAULT **p.183** BRICK **p.195**
WOOD **p.196** STUCCO **p.205** GLASS **p.206** IRON **p.208**

Gothic Revival

1740S – C.1920

KEY ARCHITECTS: AUGUSTUS PUGIN • EUGÈNE EMMANUEL VIOLLET-LE-DUC
DAVID BRYCE • EMANUELE LUIGI GALIZIA • LOUIS DELACENSERIE

After Italian artist, architect and author Giorgio Vasari (1511–74) derided the Gothic style during the Renaissance, opinions of medieval architecture went into decline.

Its rehabilitation started as early as the 1740s in Britain with Strawberry Hill, Twickenham (1749–66) designed by writer Horace Walpole (1717–97). By the 1830s, perceiving Neoclassicism as pagan, more architects began creating designs based on the seemingly more godly Gothic style, incorporating pointed arches, steep roofs, finials, lancet windows and decorative tracery, but often using different materials, for instance brick and cast iron.

Spreading across Europe, Indonesia, the Philippines, Canada and the USA, the Gothic Revival lasted until the twentieth century. In France, *The Hunchback of Notre Dame* by Victor Hugo (1802–85) was published in 1831 to draw attention to original Gothic architecture, and initiated a similar trend. Further impetus was given when Eugène Emmanuel Viollet-le-Duc (1814–79) restored Notre Dame and Amiens cathedrals between 1844–50.

In London, Charles Barry and Augustus Pugin designed the Palace of Westminster while Saint Pancras Station (1868–76) was created by George Gilbert Scott (1811–78). In New York City, the Woolworth Building (1913) was designed by Cass Gilbert (1859–1934) with Gothic detailing; for 20 years it was the tallest building in the world.

KEY DEVELOPMENTS
Designed by Friedrich Schmidt (1825–91), Vienna City Hall is predominantly built in the Gothic Revival style, with Baroque elements. Five towers, including a 98 m (322 ft) central tower, soar into the sky, while the vast brick-built building, with its limestone decorations, is arranged around seven inner courtyards and is spread over six floors.

Vienna City Hall, Friedrich Schmidt, 1872–83, Vienna, Austria

PALACE OF WESTMINSTER **p.114** ARCH **p.173** TOWER **p.174** VAULT **p.183** SPIRE **p.184** STONE **p.192** BRICK **p.195** WOOD **p.196** STAINED GLASS **p.207** IRON **p.208**

Shaker

1774
–
1900

KEY ARCHITECTS: MOSES JOHNSON • MICAJAH BURNETT
DANIEL GOODRICH

Centre Family Dwelling House,
Micajah Burnett, 1824–34,
Pleasant Hill, Kentucky, USA

The Shakers (or United Society of Believers in Christ's Second Appearing) were founded by the English-born Ann Lee (1736–84), who emigrated to America in 1774 and established the religious sect.

As Shaker communities grew, they built villages, initially in the eastern United States and gradually spreading west. By the mid-nineteenth century, there were 19 settlements and approximately 6,000 Shakers in total, mainly in New England, New York and Kentucky.

The Shaker text, *The Millennial Laws*, first written in 1821, included strict architectural rules. Living communally, Shakers built to reflect their beliefs that ornamentation such as mouldings and cornices was superfluous, that simplicity, utility, fine craftsmanship and order were paramount, and that light and cleanliness deflected evil. To this end, they incorporated numerous windows – this focus on form following function was to be advocated much later by several modernist architects.

Shaker buildings were substantial. Meeting houses were the most important, and each settlement also had a round building with a large floor space for ceremonial 'round dances'. Although early Shaker architecture was characterized by austerity and simplicity, towards the end of the nineteenth century some slightly more elaborate elements began appearing, such as bay windows, towers and porches.

KEY DEVELOPMENTS
Designed by Micajah Burnett (1791–1879) and Moses Johnson (1752–1842), the Shaker village of Pleasant Hill was occupied between 1805 and 1910. As well as following Shaker guidelines, the architecture was influenced by the popular Federal style. It had dwellings, barns and a water tower that conveyed water to the kitchens, cellars and wash houses of the village.

HANCOCK SHAKER VILLAGE **p.110** BRICK **p.195** WOOD **p.196** GLASS **p.206**

Chicago School

1879 – 1910

KEY ARCHITECTS: DANKMAR ADLER • DANIEL BURNHAM • MARTIN ROCHE
WILLIAM HOLABIRD • WILLIAM LE BARON JENNEY • LOUIS SULLIVAN

KEY DEVELOPMENTS
The Carson, Pirie, Scott and Company Building was designed by Louis Sullivan with a steel-framed structure that enabled large windows to be included, so daylight flooded into the interior. Between the windows are lightweight bands of terracotta and bronze-plated cast iron to decorate and protect the round tower. Bronze and terracotta were an unusual choice at the time, but were fire-resistant and inexpensive.

The Chicago School describes several architects active in Chicago at the turn of the twentieth century, although they were not part of any coherent group.

In the late nineteenth century, various architects and engineers in the city developed the skyscraper, generally defined at the time as a building over ten storeys high. There was no one defining style, but these architects were among the first to use the new technology of steel-frame construction, with large plate-glass windows and limited exterior ornamentation. Many Chicago School skyscrapers are based on the three parts of a classical column: the lowest floors correlate to the base, the middle storeys correspond with the shaft and the top floors are often topped with a cornice, representing the capital.

Frequently cited as the first skyscraper in the world, the Home Insurance Building was designed in 1884 by William Le Baron Jenney (1832–1907), who became known as 'the father of the American skyscraper'. Because Chicago is largely built on marshy ground, it was unable to support tall structures in the conventional way, so architects and engineers worked out innovative methods. For instance, Dankmar Adler used his experience as a military engineer to devise a foundation 'raft' of timbers, steel beams and iron I-beams.

Carson, Pirie, Scott and Company Building, Louis Sullivan, 1899, Chicago, USA

WAINWRIGHT BUILDING **p.122** TOWER **p.174** BRICK **p.195** WOOD **p.196** CONCRETE **p.201** GLASS **p.206** IRON **p.208** STEEL **p.209**

Arts and Crafts

KEY ARCHITECTS: RICHARD NORMAN SHAW • WILLIAM RICHARD LETHABY
C. F. A. VOYSEY • M. H. BAILLIE SCOTT • C. R. ASHBEE • PHILIP WEBB

Determined to move away from what they perceived as the negative effects of industrialization, several British architects and designers sought to revive craftsmanship at the end of the nineteenth century.

The Arts and Crafts movement was started by British designer, writer, artist, manufacturer and social reformer William Morris, who originally trained as an architect. Tired of the excesses of Victorian architecture and design, and believing that machines and mass production were lowering the quality of life, Morris and his followers aimed to return to a pre-industrial society. They wished to revive medieval methods of skilful, individual construction and collaborative workshops, using vernacular materials and eschewing any ornate, imposed or artificial style. Their beliefs about good design were linked to their notions of a happy society and, although much of the decorative work that emerged from the Arts and Crafts

movement was intricate and colourful, its architecture was plain and unadorned.

Also associated with the movement was the art patron, critic, draughtsman, watercolourist and philanthropist John Ruskin (1819–1900), who believed that the division of labour of the Industrial Revolution was unhealthy. After 1900, the movement spread across Europe, particularly in Germany through the creation of the Deutscher Werkbund in 1907, and in the United States, led by furniture maker Gustav Stickley (1858–1942), who founded *The Craftsman* magazine.

KEY DEVELOPMENTS
The Red House in Bexleyheath, London, was designed by the architect Philip Webb with William Morris in 1859. Using vernacular materials that are expressed honestly and undisguised, it exemplifies the early Arts and Crafts style, with red brick façades that are different from every angle, wide porches, window arches, pointed roofs, large fireplaces and an asymmetrical plan.

Red House, Philip Webb and William Morris, 1859–60, Bexleyheath, London, UK

RED HOUSE **p.116** ARCH **p.173** STONE **p.192** BRICK **p.195** WOOD **p.196** TILES **p.198**
STAINED GLASS **p.207**

Art Nouveau

1883
–
1914

KEY ARCHITECTS: HECTOR GUIMARD • HENRY VAN DE VELDE
VICTOR HORTA • OTTO WAGNER • JOSEF HOFFMANN • ANTONI GAUDÍ

KEY DEVELOPMENTS
Antoni Gaudí is the best-known practitioner of Catalan Modernism. His organic architecture shows influences from Japanese design and the Gothic Revival, and incorporates crafts including sculpture, stained glass, wrought ironwork, carpentry and trencadís (the use of mosaic-like ceramics). Often working on several projects simultaneously, Gaudí constructed Casa Batlló and Casa Milà between 1904 and 1912.

Casa Milà, Antoni Gaudí, 1906–12, Barcelona, Spain

Popular in many countries from the early 1890s until the outbreak of World War I in 1914, Art Nouveau was an influential although relatively brief art and design movement and philosophy.

It developed almost simultaneously across Europe and America, attempting to create a unique and modern expression of the age. Focusing on natural forms, asymmetry, sinuous lines and whiplash curves, architects and designers aimed to escape the excessively ornamental styles and historical replications popular during the Victorian era. They drew on a huge range of influences, including the Arts and Crafts movement, Celtic art, the Gothic Revival, Rococo, the Aesthetic movement, Symbolist art and aspects of Japanese design, often using materials such as iron

and glass. Although there are identifying characteristics, Art Nouveau also displayed many regional and national interpretations.

The style catapulted into international prominence with the 1900 Exposition Universelle in Paris. Structures built to flaunt both new technology and these new ideas at the exhibition included the dome-shaped Porte Monumentale entrance designed by René Binet (1866–1911); the brilliantly lit Palais d'Electricité by Eugène Hénard (1849–1923); the Pavillon Bleu, a grand restaurant at the foot of the Eiffel Tower designed by Gustave Serrurier-Bovy (1858–1910); and the iron and glass entrances of the Métro stations, designed by Hector Guimard (1867–1942).

SAGRADA FAMÍLIA **p.120** KARLSPLATZ UNDERGROUND STATION **p.124** DOME **p.172** ARCH **p.173** TOWER **p.174** SPIRE **p.184** BRICK **p.195** TILES **p.198** CONCRETE **p.201** IRON **p.208** STEEL **p.209**

Modernist

1900
—

KEY ARCHITECTS: ADOLF LOOS • AUGUSTE PERRET • HENRI LABROUSTE
PETER BEHRENS • ADOLF MEYER • FRANK LLOYD WRIGHT

Rejecting ornament and embracing minimalism and modern materials, Modernist architecture appeared across the world from the early twentieth century.

Inspired by such movements as Arts and Crafts, Art Nouveau, the Chicago School, the Wiener Werkstätte (established in 1903 in Vienna) and the Deutscher Werkbund (established in 1907 in Munich), Modernism developed initially in Europe, focusing on functionalism, honesty in materials and avoidance of decoration.

One early building that was to prove highly influential to Modernism was the AEG Turbine Hall, Berlin, designed by Peter Behrens in 1909, using steel, glass and stone. In 1910, the Austrian and Czech architect and theorist Adolf Loos (1870–1933) gave a lecture, *Ornament and Crime*, later published as an essay. In keeping with its argument, Loos designed Steiner House in Vienna (1910), which was

entirely devoid of ornament. Modernism reached its peak during the 1920s and 1930s with the Bauhaus and the International Style, both characterized by asymmetry, flat roofs, large windows, metal, glass, white rendering and open-plan interiors.

There were many national offshoots. In Soviet Russia, ASNOVA was founded in 1923 by architects Nikolai Ladovsky (1881–1941), Vladimir Krinsky (1890–1971) and others, who became known as 'the Rationalists' for their functional buildings.

KEY DEVELOPMENTS

Modernist architecture was associated with an analytical approach to a building's function, a rational use of materials, and the avoidance of ornament. From 1911, influenced by Behrens's AEG Turbine Hall, Walter Gropius and Adolf Meyer designed the façade of the Fagus Factory in Alfeld, Germany, employing large, flat windows and a horizontal emphasis.

Fagus Factory, Walter Gropius and Adolf Meyer, 1911–25, Alfeld, Lower Saxony, Germany

 VILLA SAVOYE **p.134** COLUMN **p.177** TERRACE **p.187** STONE **p.192** BRICK **p.195** CONCRETE **p.201** GLASS **p.206** STEEL **p.209**

Organic

KEY ARCHITECTS: FRANK LLOYD WRIGHT • BRUCE GOFF • HUGO HÄRING
IMRE MAKOVECZ • LOUIS KAHN

Frank Lloyd Wright coined the term organic architecture to describe buildings that were designed to be in harmony with their surroundings.

Explaining this approach towards the end of his life, he said, 'I'd like to have a free architecture. I'd like to have architecture that belonged where you see it standing, and was a grace to the landscape instead of a disgrace.' Wright believed that architecture should be a product of its place and time, closely connected to a particular site, and never created out of an imposed or artificial style. From 1908, he created buildings that appeared to evolve spontaneously from the environment, reflected in his choice of materials, forms and colours, echoing nature and indicating his respect for Japanese culture.

In addition, Wright felt that materials used in the architecture should not be disguised, and interior spaces should be as open as possible. He embraced new technologies, machinery and materials, and this fusion of nature and modernity, plus his creative solutions to individual problems, resulted in exceptional works of architecture. Wright's ideal influenced many others, including Santiago Calatrava (b.1951), recognized for his often sculptural designs such as the Bac de Roda Bridge (1985–7) in Barcelona and the atrium of Brookfield Place (1990) in Toronto. Jørn Utzon's Sydney Opera House is also an example of organic architecture.

KEY DEVELOPMENTS
Fallingwater adheres to Wright's principles of organic architecture. It rises on pillars from the cantilevered rock of the waterfall beneath, and echoes this natural structure in the cantilevered concrete of its balconies. It blends harmoniously with its surroundings without imitation, and its form and materials are carefully chosen to suit its environment.

Fallingwater, Frank Lloyd Wright, 1936–9, Bear Run, Pennsylvania, USA

FALLINGWATER **p.138** SYDNEY OPERA HOUSE **p.142** COLUMN **p.177** CANTILEVER **p.189** STONE **p.192**
BRICK **p.195** WOOD **p.196** CONCRETE **p.201** GLASS **p.206**

Futurist

KEY ARCHITECTS: ANTONIO SANT'ELIA • MARIO CHIATTONE
ANGIOLO MAZZONI • VIRGILIO MARCHI • OSCAR NIEMEYER

As part of the Italian Futurist movement, architect Antonio Sant'Elia (1888–1916) produced many drawings early in the twentieth century that expressed his visions for the cities of the future.

Sant'Elia's plans never reached fruition, and little Futurist architecture was ever constructed, but his designs expressed the theories of Futurism, embracing technology and the machine age, and became highly influential. Futurism began with a manifesto written by the poet Filippo Tommaso Marinetti (1876–1944) in 1909, which rejected the past, and glorified war and machines. Futurist architecture featured such characteristics as unusual angles, sharp edges, slopes, domes, sleek lines and metal components. Further manifestos followed that celebrated modern life, calling for a break with the past and an embrace of technology, war, speed and the future.

In 1912, Sant'Elia opened a design office in Milan with Mario Chiattone (1891–1957), where he created bold and vivid sketches for *La Città Nuova* (*The New City*), made up of skyscrapers with high bridges and suspended walkways. In 1914, a further manifesto, *Futurist Architecture,* was released, largely written by Sant'Elia. It outlined a new world of huge, energetic cities and stated: 'We must invent and rebuild our Futurist city like an immense and tumultuous shipyard, active, mobile, and everywhere dynamic, and the Futurist house like a gigantic machine.'

KEY DEVELOPMENTS
Sant'Elia's vision of a modern city took the form of a giant machine, and featured numerous routes at different heights, including glass and metal walkways, roads and railways. His designs were to be created with new materials, without ornament or decoration, and incorporating oblique and elliptical shapes to suggest dynamism, completely discarding the past.

La Città Nuova: Step House with Elevators from Four Street Levels, Antonio Sant'Elia, 1914

 CATHEDRAL OF BRASILIA **p.144** ARCH **p.173** TOWER **p.174** COLUMN **p.177** CANTILEVER **p.189**
STONE **p.192** BRICK **p.195** CONCRETE **p.201** GLASS **p.206** IRON **p.208** STEEL **p.209**

Expressionist

1910
–
1933

KEY ARCHITECTS: ERICH MENDELSOHN • FRITZ HÖGER • MICHEL DE KLERK
BRUNO TAUT • HANS POELZIG • HERMANN FINSTERLIN • FARIBORZ SAHBA

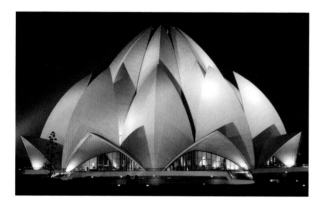

Lotus Temple, Fariborz Sahba, 1986, New Delhi, India

Between 1910 and 1924, an architectural movement developed in Germany, Austria, Denmark and elsewhere that explored human emotion, and soon became known as Expressionism.

Many Expressionist architects had fought in World War I, and their gruelling experiences had a great impact on their work. Subjective, individual and eccentric, Expressionist architecture avoided conventional building shapes and historical styles, and was often created with innovative techniques and materials. Designed to express the architect's feelings, it also sought to evoke emotional rather than intellectual responses in others.

Because they were so unique, many Expressionist buildings were never built, but appeared only as drawings, or only existed temporarily. One of the earliest and best-known was the curving Einstein Tower (1919–21) in Potsdam, Germany, designed by Erich Mendelsohn (1887–1953), which

was intended to reflect Albert Einstein's Theory of Relativity.

Because Expressionism moved away from traditional design standards, it changed the way people thought about architecture. Many architects focused on their designs as works of art, drawing their ideas from painting and sculpture rather than machines. During the 1950s and 1960s, a new version of the movement, Neo-Expressionism, developed with similar emotional and subjective ideals.

KEY DEVELOPMENTS

The Lotus Temple is a key work of Neo-Expressionist architecture. `Abdu'l-Bahá (1844–1921), the son of the founder of the Bahá'í religion, stipulated that a house of worship should be a nine-sided circular building. Inspired by the lotus flower, the architect Fariborz Sahba (b.1948) designed 27 free-standing marble-clad 'petals' in clusters of three to form nine sides.

SYDNEY OPERA HOUSE **p.142** DOME **p.172** COLUMN **p.177** BRICK **p.195** MARBLE **p.200** CONCRETE **p.201** PLASTER **p.203** GLASS **p.206** STEEL **p.209**

De Stijl

1917
–
1931

KEY ARTISTS: GERRIT RIETVELD • ROBERT VAN 'T HOFF • J. J. P. OUD
CORNELIS VAN EESTEREN • JAN WILS • THEO VAN DOESBURG

Rietveld Schröder House, Gerrit Rietveld, 1924–5, Utrecht, Netherlands

An expression of simplicity, harmony and order, De Stijl began as a universal visual language to suit the modern era.

Led by the painter and architect Theo van Doesburg (1883–1931) and the painter Piet Mondrian (1872–1944), De Stijl began as an art and design movement and journal in 1917, with the painters Vilmos Huszár (1884–1960) and Bart van der Leck (1876–1958), and the architects Robert van 't Hoff (1887–1979) and J. J. P. Oud (1890–1963). Architect Gerrit Rietveld joined in 1918.

The movement was intended to express an ideal fusion of form and function through a reduction of elements to basic forms and colours, including only vertical and horizontal angles, and only black, white, grey and primary colours. Evolving from Cubism, the movement focused on geometric forms and emphasized balance and harmony. De Stijl's architectural ideas were influenced by the Dutch architect

Hendrik Berlage (1856–1934) and particularly by Frank Lloyd Wright.

The movement's architectural characteristics include flat roofs, plain windows, defined vertical and horizontal planes, and surfaces painted white or grey with highlights of blue, yellow and red. De Stijl soon expanded, with all members aiming to achieve harmonious forms, and its architecture became an important precursor to Bauhaus and International Style architecture.

KEY DEVELOPMENTS
The Rietveld Schröder House was built by Gerrit Rietveld adhering to the ideals of De Stijl, including a complete break from all previous architectural styles. Commissioned by Truus Schröder-Schräder who wanted it to be 'grand and open', the house is asymmetrical with vertical and horizontal planes, and nearly all the interior walls can be moved to open it up inside.

RIETVELD SCHRÖDER HOUSE **p.128** WINDOW **p.167** TERRACE **p.187** BRICK **p.195** CONCRETE **p.201**
PLASTER **p.203** GLASS **p.206** STEEL **p.209**

International Style

1918 — 1939

KEY ARCHITECTS: LE CORBUSIER • RICHARD NEUTRA • PHILIP JOHNSON
CHARLOTTE PERRIAND • EILEEN GRAY • RUDOLPH SCHINDLER

Villa E-1027,
Eileen Gray,
1926–9,
Roquebrune-
Cap-Martin,
France

The International Style emerged in Europe after World War One, influenced by recent movements, including De Stijl and Streamline Moderne, and had a close relationship to the Bauhaus.

The antithesis of nearly every other architectural movement that preceded it, the International Style eliminated extraneous ornament and used modern industrial materials such as steel, glass, reinforced concrete and chrome. Rectilinear, flat-roofed, asymmetrical and white, it became a symbol of modernity across the world. It seemed to offer a crisp, clean, rational future after the horrors of war.

Named by the architect Philip Johnson and historian Henry-Russell Hitchcock (1903–87) in 1932, the movement was epitomized by Charles-Edouard Jeanneret, or Le Corbusier, and was clearly expressed in his statement that 'a house is a machine for living in'. In 1914, he patented some prototype buildings made of reinforced concrete called Dom-ino Houses that were supported on pilotis, and in 1923, he published *Vers une Architecture* (*Towards an Architecture*), explaining his 'Five Points of a New Architecture'. Among these were his beliefs that there should be ribbon windows, or at least a horizontal emphasis, freely arranged interior walls, pilotis and a flat roof or roof garden. He designed several villas around Paris exemplifying these theories during the 1920s, including the Villa Savoye.

KEY DEVELOPMENTS
Designed and built by the architect and furniture designer Eileen Gray (1878–1976) at a time when it was difficult for women to break into the male-dominated world of architecture, the white, L-shaped Villa E-1027 has large, unadorned windows, minimal decoration and an open-plan interior. Gray also designed the house's furniture.

VILLA SAVOYE **p.134** PORTICO/PORCH **p.186** PILOTI **p.188** CANTILEVER **p.189** BRICK **p.195** CONCRETE **p.201** STUCCO **p.205** GLASS **p.206** STEEL **p.209**

Bauhaus

1919
—
1933

KEY ARCHITECTS: WALTER GROPIUS • HANNES MEYER • HANS WITTWER
LUDWIG MIES VAN DER ROHE • MART STAM • MARCEL BREUER

Founded in 1919 by Walter Gropius, the Bauhaus was a profoundly influential German design school that taught a broad range of skills in art and design, and in methods of industrial production.

Bauhaus students were taught a total design approach that encompassed everything from architecture to painting, from ceramics to furniture design, from typography to textile design and more. The school existed in three German cities under three different architect-directors: from 1919 to 1925 in Weimar under Walter Gropius; from 1925 to 1932 in Dessau, where Hannes Meyer (1889–1954) took over in 1928, until he was replaced by Ludwig Mies van der Rohe in 1930, who oversaw the move to Berlin in 1932.

Although architecture was not taught until 1927 and the school was closed by the Nazi regime in 1933, staff and students continued to practise its idealistic precepts throughout their careers, helping to shape Modernism across the world. Through the study of form and materials, students became experts at understated expression, creating architecture that emphasizes function, utility, clean lines and an absence of superfluous decoration. Most Bauhaus buildings are concrete-built, geometric and flat-roofed, with large, metal-framed windows and a reduced colour scheme.

László Moholy-Nagy's House, Walter Gropius, 1925–6, Dessau, Germany

KEY DEVELOPMENTS

At the Bauhaus in Dessau, Gropius designed a complex of buildings, including three pairs of semi-detached Bauhaus masters' houses. Built as interlocking structures of different heights, the houses are partially constructed with prefabricated components and include plain windows and balconies, large windows and coloured or grey accents. This example was built for László Moholy-Nagy (1895–1946).

BAUHAUS BUILDING **p.130** SEAGRAM BUILDING **p.140** WINDOW **p.167** TERRACE **p.187** CANTILEVER **p.189** CONCRETE **p.201** GLASS **p.206** STEEL **p.209**

Art Deco

1925
—
1940

KEY ARCHITECTS: WALTER TEAGUE • HOWARD ROBERTSON
WILLIAM F. LAMB • YASUO MATSUI • WILLIAM VAN ALEN • THOMAS WALLIS

Empire State Building, Shreve, Lamb and
Harmon, 1929–31, New York City, USA

An international art, design and architectural style, Art Deco was named retrospectively after an exhibition held in Paris in 1925, and encompassed furniture, textiles, ceramics, ornaments, painting, sculpture and architecture.

Although it ended with the start of World War II, its appeal has endured. Elements of the style drew on ancient Egyptian, Greek, Roman, African, Aztec and Japanese influences, but also on Futurism, Cubism and the Bauhaus. An expression of glamour, energy and modernity, Art Deco's architectural features include columns, pediments, arches and spires, with a geometric emphasis. Bold colour was often applied, as were embellishments such as low-relief designs and angular patterns and shapes, for instance chevrons, ziggurats and sun rays. Predominant materials include chrome, brass, polished steel and aluminium, inlaid wood, stone and stained glass.

First used in public and commercial buildings, the style spread to domestic architecture, often with curved walls, arches, brightly coloured stained glass, vitrolite tiles and large windows. Art Deco evolved into Streamline Moderne, or Art Moderne, which had a more pared-down aesthetic, incorporating curves, clean lines and minimal decoration, which developed out of the glamour and style of cruise liners and the polished efficiency of machines.

KEY DEVELOPMENTS

Designed by the firm Shreve, Lamb and Harmon, the Empire State Building in New York City is a 103-storey, limestone-clad Art Deco skyscraper. Completed in 1931, the stylized, geometric 443 m (1,454 ft) tall building is stepped at the top, resembling an ancient ziggurat. For over 40 years, it was the tallest building in the world.

CHRYSLER BUILDING **p.132** ARCH **p.173** TOWER **p.174** COLUMN **p.177** ATRIUM **p.180** SPIRE **p.184**
MARBLE **p.200** CONCRETE **p.201** GLASS **p.206** IRON **p.208** STEEL **p.209** ALUMINIUM **p.210**

Geodesic

KEY ARCHITECTS: RICHARD BUCKMINSTER FULLER • WALTHER BAUERSFELD
THOMAS C. HOWARD

Geodesic domes are thin, shell-like hemispherical structures, composed of a network of straight lines that creates a lattice, usually of rigid triangles.

This provides a strong, lightweight framework that enables them to withstand heavy loads. The possibilities of geodesic architecture were vigorously promoted by the American engineer and architect Richard Buckminster Fuller from the 1940s, although the style was invented earlier. The first geodesic dome was designed by the German engineer Walther Bauersfeld (1879–1959), who started working on a design for a planetarium in 1912 while working for the Carl Zeiss optical company. Progress was halted by World War I, but it resumed shortly afterwards, and the project was installed at the company's headquarters in Jena in 1923.

Between the wars, Bauersfeld developed more examples in Germany and America, yet it was not until the 1940s that Buckminster Fuller named the domes 'geodesic'. He received a US patent in June 1954, and the US Marines began experimenting with geodesic domes that could be delivered by helicopter.

Exceptionally strong for its weight and capable of being constructed very quickly, this style of architecture was used for a number of special purposes, such as auditoriums, weather observatories and storage facilities. For the 1964 World's Fair in New York City, a geodesic dome was built as a pavilion, designed by Thomas C. Howard (b.1931) of Synergetics, Inc. In October 1982, one of Buckminster Fuller's most famous geodesic domes, Spaceship Earth at the EPCOT Center in Walt Disney World, Florida, was completed.

Montreal Biosphere, Richard Buckminster Fuller and Shoji Sadao, 1967, Montreal, Canada

KEY DEVELOPMENTS
The former American Pavilion at the 1967 World's Fair in Montreal, Canada, is a geodesic dome designed by Buckminster Fuller and Shoji Sadao (b.1927). Now a museum known as the Montreal Biosphere and dedicated to the environment, it is made of layers of steel rods that make triangular and hexagonal structures, each sealed with acrylic sheets.

MONTREAL BIOSPHERE **p.148** DOME **p.172** ATRIUM **p.180** CONCRETE **p.201** STEEL **p.209** ALUMINIUM **p.210** PLASTIC **p.211**

Brutalist

1952
–
1975

KEY ARCHITECTS: PAUL RUDOLPH • ERNŐ GOLDFINGER • ALISON SMITHSON
PETER SMITHSON • RODNEY GORDON • CLORINDO TESTA • HANS ASPLUND

São Paulo Museum of Art,
Lina Bo Bardi, 1956–68,
São Paulo, Brazil

Based on social equality, Brutalism was inspired by Le Corbusier's 1947–52 Unité d'Habitation in Marseilles.

It seems the term was originally coined by Swedish architect Hans Asplund (1921–94), but Le Corbusier's use of the description *béton brut*, meaning raw concrete, for his choice of material for the Unité d'Habitation was particularly influential. The architects Alison Smithson (1928–93) and Peter Smithson (1923–2003) soon adopted the name, and it was generally accepted by the time that architectural critic Reyner Banham (1922–88) published the book *The New Brutalism* in 1966.

The style flourished from the 1950s to the mid-1970s, mainly using concrete, which although not new in itself, was unconventional when exposed on façades. Before Brutalism, concrete was usually hidden beneath other materials. Its exposed

use in Brutalism, coupled with a complete absence of ornamentation, suggested honesty: nothing was hidden or disguised.

Bulky, solid-looking, quite formidable and often featuring repeated modular elements, most Brutalist architecture was created for government or institutional buildings, such as tower blocks, university buildings and shopping centres. The Smithsons and Ernő Goldfinger (1902–87) were among the earliest proponents of the style, which appeared in some form in many countries around the world.

KEY DEVELOPMENTS

A landmark of modern architecture in Brazil, São Paulo Museum of Art (MASP) was designed by Lina Bo Bardi (1914–92) on the stipulation that the building should not block the site's scenic views. She created a solution that was both simple and powerful, suspending its vast concrete and glass structure and leaving open ground beneath.

HABITAT 67 **p.146** COLUMN **p.177** TERRACE **p.187** BRICK **p.195** CONCRETE **p.201** GLASS **p.206** STEEL **p.209**

Postmodern

1964 – 1999

KEY ARCHITECTS: ROBERT VENTURI • DENISE SCOTT BROWN • MICHAEL GRAVES • PHILIP JOHNSON • HANS HOLLEIN • ALDO ROSSI • CHARLES MOORE

Piazza d'Italia, Charles Moore, 1978, New Orleans, USA

KEY DEVELOPMENTS

The idea of 'inclusive' architecture that can be enjoyed by anyone was championed by Charles Moore (1925–93). He designed the Piazza d'Italia in New Orleans in honour of the city's Italian citizens, featuring brightly coloured colonnades, arches and a bell tower, embellished in places with neon and metallics, all placed in a curve around an exotic-looking fountain.

No one definable style, Postmodernism is an eclectic mix of approaches that appeared in the late twentieth century in reaction against Modernism, which was increasingly perceived as monotonous and conservative.

As with many movements, a complete antithesis to Modernism developed. In 1966, the architect Robert Venturi (1925–2018) had published his book, *Complexity and Contradiction in Architecture*, which praised the originality and creativity of the Mannerist and Baroque architecture of Rome, and encouraged more ambiguity and complexity in contemporary design. Complaining about the austerity and tedium of so many smooth steel and glass Modernist buildings, and in deliberate denunciation of the famous Modernist maxim 'Less is more', Venturi stated 'Less is a bore'. His theories became a major influence on the development of

Postmodernism. At around the same time, at various places across the world, Postmodern architects created brash, irreverent and witty designs that they felt were liberating after so many years of pared down, clean-lined Modernism.

They also used modern materials and unexpected techniques to help create individual, surprising buildings, including perhaps the first postmodernist building, the Vanna Venturi House by Robert Venturi and Denise Scott Brown (b.1931), completed in 1964, and the most important postmodern building in London, No. 1 Poultry by James Stirling (1926–92), completed in 1997 after his death.

PORTLAND BUILDING **p.152** WINDOW **p.167** CHIMNEY **p.169** ARCH **p.173** TOWER **p.174** COLUMN **p.177** BUTTRESS **p.178** GABLE **p.179** BRICK **p.195** CONCRETE **p.201** GLASS **p.206** STEEL **p.209**

Minimalist

1960
—

KEY ARCHITECTS: TADAO ANDO • LUIS BARRAGÁN • JOHN PAWSON • RYUE NISHIZAWA • KAZUYO SEJIMA • ALBERTO CAMPO BAEZA • CLAUDIO SILVESTRIN

KEY DEVELOPMENTS
Built on an industrial heritage site in Essen, Germany, the School of Management and Design was designed by Kazuyo Sejima and Ryue Nishizawa for SANAA. It appears to be simply a massive cube of concrete. Yet despite the plain simplicity of its exterior, the interior spaces are extremely varied, including diverse ceiling heights.

Zollverein School of Management and Design, SANAA, 2005–06, Essen, Germany

Retaining their focus on functionalism and clarity, Minimalist architecture developed out of De Stijl, the Bauhaus and the International Style.

At its height during the late 1960s and 1970s, Minimalism aimed to achieve not just the reduction of forms but of all elements. The movement was heavily influenced by traditional Japanese architecture, which pares back elements and avoids the superfluous. With its concern for simplified form, space and materials, Minimalist architecture abridges the design elements, and avoids ornamentation or decoration. Once all elements have been condensed in this manner, all that remains of any Minimalist work of architecture is the 'essence'.

Although most architects seek to harmonize buildings with their surroundings, Minimalists use this as their starting point and primary focus. This is exemplified by Tadao Ando (b.1941), who blends traditional Japanese concepts with his own personal expression, combining geometry and nature. His usual materials are concrete or wood, and his forms are purposefully austere and geometric, shaped to maximize space and light. Another Japanese architect, Kazuyo Sejima, works both independently and in collaboration with Ryue Nishizawa as SANAA. Her designs often feature thin sections and transparent elements.

MORIYAMA HOUSE **p.156** ATRIUM **p.180** CANTILEVER **p.189** STONE **p.192** GLASS **p.206** STEEL **p.209** ALUMINIUM **p.210** TITANIUM **p.215**

High-tech

1970

KEY ARCHITECTS: NORMAN FOSTER • RICHARD ROGERS • RENZO PIANO
MICHAEL HOPKINS • JEAN NOUVEL • SANTIAGO CALATRAVA

Influenced by engineering, new technology and machines, High-tech architecture celebrates and exposes the construction of buildings.

The movement – sometimes called Bowellism or Structural Expressionism – began in the early 1970s, when some architects integrated the latest industrial and technological components onto the exterior structures of their buildings, combining them with lightweight, smooth materials, especially steel, aluminium and glass.

In some ways, High-tech developed out of Modernism; in other ways, it was a reaction against it, embracing the decorative possibilities of pipes, air ducts, escalators, lifts and other services and elements that would normally be hidden within the internal structure. Perhaps the most famous example of this approach is the Pompidou Centre in Paris (1971–7), designed by Renzo Piano and Richard Rogers who, with Norman Foster, were among the earliest proponents of the style.

As well as these expressive, industrial-looking exteriors, High-tech architecture usually features flexible interiors and often an unexpected use of colour. Overall, the style focused on the concept of showing how technology can improve the world by dramatizing and drawing attention to technical features, and by exploring such constructional elements as cantilevering, ribbon windows, concrete towers, curved walls, exposed steel structures, visible air-conditioning ducts, service modules, movable partitions and plug-in service pods.

KEY DEVELOPMENTS
When Norman Foster's HSBC Building in Hong Kong was completed, it was the most expensive building in the world. Extremely innovative, it has no internal supporting structure. Its vast ten-storey atrium is lit by a mirrored central sun-scoop, thus sunlight provides one of the main sources of lighting. This also helps to conserve energy, as do sun shades fitted on the exterior.

HSBC Building, Foster and Partners, 1983–6, Hong Kong

POMPIDOU CENTRE **p.150** WINDOW **p.167** TOWER **p.174** ATRIUM **p.180** PORTICO/PORCH **p.186**
TERRACE **p.187** CANTILEVER **p.189** GLASS **p.206** STEEL **p.209** ALUMINIUM **p.210**

Sustainable

1970

KEY ARCHITECTS: KEN YEANG • ERIC COREY FREED • WILLIAM MCDONOUGH
ROLF DISCH • EUGENE PANDALA • GLENN MURCUTT • STEFANO BOERI

Fujisawa Sustainable Smart Town, various architects,
2010–14, Kanagawa Prefecture, Fujisawa, Japan

Using only environmentally friendly techniques and materials, Sustainable architecture seeks to minimize the negative impact of buildings on the environment.

Often called 'green architecture', it first appeared in the late 1960s when awareness of human damage to our ecosystem became increasingly widespread. To address these concerns, some architects began exploring several approaches. Overall, the architecture seeks to minimize the environmental impact of buildings by efficiency and moderation in the use of materials and the consumption of energy. Energy efficiency over the entire life cycle of a building becomes the most important objective. This is achieved by such things as using natural, ethically sourced and recyclable materials; conserving heat through efficient insulation; using alternative or renewable energy sources; and using passive solar heating and ventilation to reduce dependency on fossil fuels and air conditioning.

Although Sustainable architecture is more about content and function than about form, the materials are often unconventional (for instance bamboo, wood, rock and carbon fibre), as are the processes employed. As a result, many Sustainable buildings are also highly innovative and unusual in appearance, for instance the layered Dutch Pavilion by MVRDV at Expo 2000 in Hanover.

KEY DEVELOPMENTS
The aim of the pioneering Fujisawa Sustainable Smart Town near Tokyo is to create an entirely sustainable town in an earthquake zone. Every house has sustainable technology, including solar panels and a fuel processor, all connected by a smart grid. Even the leaf-inspired road layout channels air along every street, reducing the need for air conditioning.

BOSCO VERTICALE **p.158** WINDOW **p.167** ROOF **p.168** COURTYARD **p.175** PORTICO/PORCH **p.186**
WOOD **p.196** BAMBOO **p.199** GLASS **p.206** CARBON FIBRE **p.212** RECYCLED MATERIALS **p.213**

Deconstructivist

1980
–
2005

KEY ARCHITECTS: FRANK GEHRY • DANIEL LIBESKIND • REM KOOLHAAS
PETER EISENMAN • ZAHA HADID • BERNARD TSCHUMI • WOLF D. PRIX

Characterized by the manipulation of structure, surfaces and shapes, Deconstructivism focused on freedom of forms more than functional constraints.

From the late 1970s to the early twenty-first century, Deconstructivist buildings appeared in various parts of the world, challenging expectations and perceptions of what architecture should be. Many appear fractured yet were planned and executed with precision. Some Deconstructivist buildings seem illogical and incoherent, while others convey harmony and fluidity. Most impart a sense of fragmentation and unpredictability, along with an absence of symmetry. Partially influenced by Postmodernism, the movement was also inspired by Constructivism and Futurism, and by the theories of the French philosopher Jacques Derrida (1930–2004), who argued that meaning exists because of relationships, for instance hard exists because of soft: we know what things are because we know what they are not, and meanings of things change over time.

As a result, Deconstructivist architecture often goes against what is expected. For instance, it may include diagonals and unexpected shapes. An archetypal work of Deconstructivism is the fluid, shiny Guggenheim Museum (1992–7) in Bilbao (see page 215) designed by Frank Gehry (b.1929). Another is the Dancing House (1992–6) in Prague, also by Gehry in collaboration with Vlado Milunić (b.1941), which contrasts dramatically with Prague's historic architecture.

KEY DEVELOPMENTS
In 1988, Daniel Libeskind (b.1946) was chosen as the designer of a major extension for the Jewish Museum in Berlin. His radical ideas project feelings of absence, emptiness and invisibility, echoing the effects of the Holocaust on the Jewish people in Berlin and beyond. The zigzag-shaped building has no exterior door; entry and exit are through an underground corridor.

Jewish Museum, Daniel Libeskind, 1992–9, Berlin, Germany

VITRA FIRE STATION **p.154** ATRIUM **p.180** CANTILEVER **p.189** STONE **p.192** GLASS **p.206** STEEL **p.209** ALUMINIUM **p.210** TITANIUM **p.215**

THE BUILDINGS

GREAT PYRAMID 54 • **PARTHENON** ICTINUS, CALLIKRATES AND PHIDIAS 56 • **SANCHI STUPA** 58 • **PANTHEON** 60 • **HAGIA SOPHIA** ISIDORE AND ANTHEMIUS 62 • **TEMPLE OF INSCRIPTIONS** 64 • **DOME OF THE ROCK** RAJA IBN HAYWAH AND YAZID IBN SALLAM 68 • **PRAMBANAN** 70 • **MARIA LAACH ABBEY** 72 • **ANGKOR WAT** 74 • **KRAK DES CHEVALIERS** 76 • **CHARTRES CATHEDRAL** 78 • **ALHAMBRA** 80 • **SANTA MARIA DEL FIORE** ARNOLFO DI CAMBIO AND FILIPPO BRUNELLESCHI 82 • **DOGE'S PALACE** FILIPPO CALENDARIO 86 • **TEMPLE OF THE SUN** 88 • **SAINT PETER'S BASILICA** DONATO BRAMANTE AND MICHELANGELO BUONARROTI 90 • **SHIBAM** 92 • **SAINT BASIL'S CATHEDRAL** BARMA AND POSTNIK YAKOVLEV 94 • **VILLA LA ROTONDA** ANDREA PALLADIO 96 • **TAJ MAHAL** USTAD AHMAD LAHORI 98 • **RINSHUNKAKU** 100 • **PALACE OF VERSAILLES** LOUIS LE VAU AND JULES HARDOUIN-MANSART 102 • **SAINT PAUL'S CATHEDRAL** CHRISTOPHER WREN 106 • **WIESKIRCHE** DOMINIKUS ZIMMERMANN AND JOHANN BAPTIST ZIMMERMANN 108 • **HANCOCK SHAKER VILLAGE** 110 • **CAPITOL BUILDING** WILLIAM THORNTON AND THOMAS USTICK WALTER 112 • **PALACE OF WESTMINSTER** CHARLES BARRY AND AUGUSTUS PUGIN 114 • **RED HOUSE** • PHILIP WEBB AND WILLIAM MORRIS 116 • **NEUSCHWANSTEIN CASTLE** EDUARD RIEDEL AND GEORG VON DOLLMANN 118 • **SAGRADA FAMÍLIA** ANTONI GAUDÍ 120 • **WAINWRIGHT BUILDING** LOUIS SULLIVAN AND DANKMAR ADLER 122 • **KARLSPLATZ UNDERGROUND STATION** OTTO WAGNER 124 • **GREAT MOSQUE OF DJENNÉ** 126 • **RIETVELD SCHRÖDER HOUSE** GERRIT RIETVELD 128 **BAUHAUS BUILDING** WALTER GROPIUS 130 • **CHRYSLER BUILDING** WILLIAM VAN ALEN 132 • **VILLA SAVOYE** LE CORBUSIER AND PIERRE JEANNERET 134 • **FALLINGWATER** FRANK LLOYD WRIGHT 138 • **SEAGRAM BUILDING** LUDWIG MIES VAN DER ROHE 140 • **SYDNEY OPERA HOUSE** JØRN UTZON 142 • **CATHEDRAL OF BRASILIA** OSCAR NIEMEYER 144 • **HABITAT 67** MOSHE SAFDIE 146 • **MONTREAL BIOSPHERE** BUCKMINSTER FULLER 148 • **POMPIDOU CENTRE** RICHARD ROGERS AND RENZO PIANO 150 • **PORTLAND BUILDING** MICHAEL GRAVES 152 • **VITRA FIRE STATION** ZAHA HADID 154 • **MORIYAMA HOUSE** RYUE NISHIZAWA 156 • **BOSCO VERTICALE** STEFANO BOERI ARCHITETTI 158 • **ELBPHILHARMONIE** HERZOG & DE MEURON 160

Great Pyramid

GIZA, EGYPT

c.2589
–
2566 BCE

ANCIENT EGYPTIAN **p.12**

Other key works
Step Pyramid of Zoser, architect unknown, c.2650 BCE, Sakkara, Egypt
Red Pyramid of Sneferu, architect unknown, c.2600 BCE, Cairo, Egypt
Pyramid of Khafre, architect unknown, c.2570 BCE, Giza, Egypt

Of the three straight-sided pyramids at Giza built as tombs for the kings of the Old and Middle Kingdoms, the Great Pyramid, also known as the Pyramid of Khufu or the Pyramid of Cheops, is the oldest and largest.

Constructed as a tomb for the Pharaoh Khufu, who reigned from 2589 to 2566 BCE, the Great Pyramid followed contemporary design in achieving a great height, pointing up to the gods and creating a commanding presence across the land. Originally covered by smooth white-limestone casing stones, it was the tallest man-made structure in the world for more than 3,800 years. Massive, yet precision-built, the pyramid is 146.5 metres (481 feet) high, and made with an estimated 2.3 million limestone blocks. The white casing stones came from nearby quarries across the river, but some of the largest granite stones came from Aswan, over 804 kilometres (500 miles) away. Gypsum mortar held the blocks together and the peak was probably topped with gold. It is estimated that 5.5 million tonnes of limestone, 8,000 tonnes of granite and 500,000 tonnes of mortar were used in the construction, which took between ten and twenty years. There are three known chambers inside, reached by narrow passages. The lowest chamber is cut into the bedrock upon which the pyramid was built and was never finished, while the 'Queen's Chamber' and 'King's Chamber' are located higher.

PYRAMID ARCHITECTURE
From around 2650 BCE, pyramids were built as tombs for ancient Egyptian nobles. The first were stepped, and in accordance with religious beliefs, all were constructed on the west bank of the Nile where the sun sets. Tens of thousands of workers were hired to build them, and while construction was in progress they were lodged in huge encampments nearby.

STONE **p.192** PLASTER **p.203**

Parthenon

ICTINUS • CALLIKRATES • PHIDIAS: ATHENS, GREECE

447
–
432 BCE

High on the Acropolis above Athens, the Parthenon was built to house a statue of the goddess Athena and to proclaim the city's success in defeating invading armies.

The Parthenon was designed by the architects Ictinus and Callikrates (both active mid-5th century BCE), and its construction was overseen by the architect and sculptor Phidias (c.480–430 BCE), who also designed the huge statue – the Athena Parthenos – for the central *cella* (shrine). No previous Greek temple had been so sumptuously decorated, with its copious sculptures and an unprecedented 22,000 tonnes of white marble from the nearby Mount Pentelicus.

Its design mixed two architectural styles – Doric and Ionic – and made considerable use of a 4:9 ratio. This appears in the relation between the diameter of the columns and the spaces between them; between the height of the building and its width; and between the width of the inner *cella* and its length. Other techniques made the building appear perfectly proportioned and gave the illusion of straight lines when seen from a distance, including the use of entasis, in which columns bulge slightly in the middle. The columns are in an unusual arrangement, with eight at the front and seventeen along the side, and are also narrower and closer together than in other contemporary temples. A sculptural frieze originally ran round the entire building, while the roof was constructed using cedar beams and marble tiles.

ICTINUS, CALLIKRATES AND PHIDIAS

According to Plutarch, Ictinus, Callikrates and Phidias worked on several other temples throughout Greece. Callikrates worked mainly in Athens during the great building programme instigated by the statesman and general Pericles (494–429 BCE). Phidias was celebrated for his sculpture and acted as supervisor for all the architectural and artistic works for the Acropolis.

ANCIENT GREEK **p.14**

Other key works

Temple of Aphaia, architect unknown, c.490 BCE, Aegina, Greece
Temple of Hephaestus, architect unknown, c.449 BCE, Athens, Greece
Erechtheion, architect unknown, c.406 BCE, Athens, Greece

COLUMN **p.177** PORTICO/PORCH **p.186** WOOD **p.196** MARBLE **p.200**

Sanchi Stupa

MADHYA PRADESH STATE, INDIA

C.300
—
100 BCE

STUPA ARCHITECTURE

Although there are regional variations, all stupas have three fundamental features. First is the *anda*, or hemispherical dome with a solid core. Deep inside the *anda* is a relic chamber called the *tabena*. Second is the *harmika* or square railing, and third is a central pillar supporting an umbrella-like form, the *chatra*, that protects the dome from the elements.

BUDDHIST **p.15**

The Great Stupa at Sanchi in central India served as an architectural prototype for all other stupas that followed.

One of the largest and oldest stone structures in India, Sanchi Stupa was first built in the third century BCE by the Mauryan emperor Ashoka (304–232 BCE). It was later expanded to twice its initial size in stone. Traditionally believed to have been built over the relics of the Buddha, the central structure is a solid brick hemispherical dome (*anda*) on a stone platform that was originally coated in a layer of smooth plaster. Recesses were included for lamps to be lit on religious festivals as, among other things, the dome symbolizes heaven curving over the Earth. A raised terrace with a railing encircles the dome's base, where the faithful circumambulate in a clockwise direction.

The entire structure is enclosed by a low wall (*vedika*), which contains four ceremonial gateways (*torana*) at the four cardinal points. These were added in the first century CE. Each gateway consists of two squared posts with capitals of sculptured animals or dwarfs topped by three architraves. All areas of the building are covered with reliefs depicting events of the Buddha's life, stories about the Buddha's previous lives, scenes of early Buddhism, and other related symbols. At the top, the parasol-like structure, or *chatra*, symbolizes the building's high status.

Other key works
Borobudur, architect unknown, 9th century CE, Borobudur, Java, Indonesia

Amaravati Stupa, architect unknown, 3rd century BCE–c.250 CE, Amaravathi, Andhra Pradesh, India

Ruwanwelisaya, architect unknown, 137 BCE, Anuradhapura, Sri Lanka

DOME **p.172** STONE **p.192** BRICK **p.195** PLASTER **p.203**

Pantheon

ROME, ITALY

C.114
–
124 CE

Famous for its massive entrance portico and colossal circular dome, the Pantheon in Rome is the best preserved of all Roman temples.

Still the largest unreinforced concrete dome in the world and remarkable for its unique proportions and engineering achievements, the Pantheon was probably started during the reign of Emperor Trajan (53–117 CE) and finished during the reign of Emperor Hadrian (76–138 CE), covering a previous temple erected in 27 BCE. The exterior, fronted by a portico with eight granite Corinthian columns across and three deep, leads to a huge circular, richly decorated chamber, or *cella*. Formed with a series of arches, this is an open, airy and unified space, while the *cella* in previous temples was usually rectangular.

The dome is a half-sphere with a 44.3 metre (144 foot) diameter, which is exactly equal to its floor-to-summit height. Sunken panels or coffers in the dome add interest and reduce its weight as it bears down on to the wide surrounding brick wall. When the bronze doors are closed, the oculus at the dome's centre is the only source of light. Pantheon means 'all the gods' and in 609 CE it became the first temple to be consecrated as a Catholic church. Renamed Santa Maria ad Martyres, the remains of many Christian martyrs were brought from Rome's catacombs and buried beneath its floor.

Other key works
Maison Carrée, architect unknown, 2nd century CE, Nîmes, France
Temple of Bacchus, architect unknown, 150–250 CE, Baalbek, Lebanon
Temple of Hadrian, architect unknown, 145 CE, Rome, Italy

ANCIENT ROMAN **p.16**

ROMAN ARCHITECTS

Highly respected, Roman architects built prolifically. Their jobs amalgamated engineering, surveying and architecture. One of the greatest was Marco Vitruvius Pollio (c.75–c.15 BCE) who worked for Julius Caesar (100–44 BCE), building numerous structures and writing the treatise *De Architectura* that explained architecture as a unification of arts and sciences and influenced other architects for centuries.

DOME **p.172** ARCH **p.173** COURTYARD **p.175** COLUMN **p.177** VAULT **p.183** PORTICO/PORCH **p.186**
STONE **p.192** BRICK **p.195** MARBLE **p.200** CONCRETE **p.201**

Hagia Sophia

ISIDORE • ANTHEMIUS: ISTANBUL, TURKEY

C.532 – 537 CE

Other key works

Santa Sabina, architect unknown, 422–432 CE, Rome, Italy

Hagia Eirene, architect unknown, 548 CE, Istanbul, Turkey

Sant'Apollinare in Classe, architect unknown, 549 CE, Ravenna, Italy

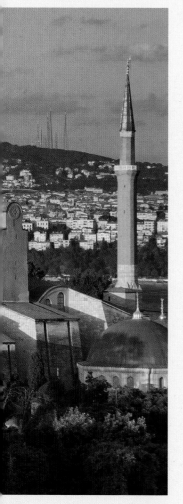

After the fall of Rome in the fifth century, the eastern part of the Roman empire survived, ruled by a succession of Christian emperors who were based in the capital city of Constantinople (present-day Istanbul).

The first church of Hagia Sophia (Divine Wisdom) was built in 326 CE by Emperor Constantine (272–337 CE) as part of the newly founded Constantinople, but it was later ordered to be rebuilt by the Emperor Justinian (c.482–565 CE). With its enormous dome measuring 32.5 metres (107 foot) wide and 56 metres (184 foot) high, the church became the prototype for much Byzantine architecture that followed. Justinian chose physicist Isidore of Miletus (c.442–c.537 CE) and mathematician Anthemius of Tralles (c.474–c.534 CE) as the architects, although Anthemius died before the church was completed.

Taking just five years to complete, the massive building contains a vast space for worship created by its dome, which is supported by four curved pendentive vaults on four towering arches. It was the first dome to be built using this pendentive device. Around the walls are 40 clerestory windows, allowing light to flood in, while aisles running around the building are screened with colonnades. Two semi-domes, equal in diameter to the main dome, were added later, working as buttresses for the main dome. In the sixteenth century, after the building was turned from a church into a mosque, minarets of brick and stone were added.

ISIDORE OF MILETUS AND ANTHEMIUS OF TRALLES
Before designing Hagia Sophia, Isidore of Miletus taught stereometry and physics at the universities of Alexandria and Constantinople. He also studied the work of the Greek physicist, inventor and mathematician Archimedes (c.287–c.212 BCE), and wrote a commentary on vaulting. Anthemius worked as a mathematician, physicist and engineer.

DOME **p.172** ARCH **p.173** COLUMN **p.177** VAULT **p.183** PORTICO/PORCH **p.186** STONE **p.192** BRICK **p.195** MOSAIC **p.204** GLASS **p.206**

Temple of Inscriptions

PALENQUE, MEXICO

c.670
–
700 CE

The Temple of the Inscriptions at the seventh-century Mayan site of Palenque is the largest Mesoamerican stepped pyramid structure.

Exemplifying Mayan temple structure, the Temple of the Inscriptions was built as the funerary monument for a seventh-century ruler of Palenque, K'inich Janaab' Pakal (603–83 CE). The original city of Palenque was sacked in 599 CE, and Pakal's ambitious rebuilding included his own mausoleum. Its completion took years, involving hundreds of labourers, masons, artists and stone workers. Pakal's son and successor K'inich Kan B'alam II (635–702 CE) continued the work, including Pakal's intricately carved sarcophagus.

With nine exterior levels representing the nine levels of Xibalba, the Maya underworld, the pyramid is rich in symbolic meaning. A single steep staircase rises to a top platform, which is surmounted by the temple itself containing several chambers. Inside, a 13-level secret passageway descends to Pakal's tomb, representing the

Above: Originally covered in brightly coloured stucco, the temple was situated close to the Royal Palace in Palenque, indicating its prestige.

Right: Broad stone steps lead to the top of the pyramid. Although they are wide, this generosity was to show the importance of the temple, as they were only used by Mayan priests and the royal family.

Other key works
Pyramid of the Sun, architect
unknown, c.200–50 CE,
Teotihuacan, Mexico
Temple of the Giant Jaguar,
architect unknown, 730 CE, Tikal,
Guatemala
Temple of the Warriors, architect
unknown, c.1100, Yucatan, Mexico

Left: The four piers at the front of the
temple were decorated with stucco
reliefs of Mayan gods, spirit ancestors
and Mayan rulers, but the inscriptions
that have given the temple its name are
mainly inside.

13 levels of the Mayan heavens. Pakal's sarcophagus has a
stone lid carved with hieroglyphs chronicling his life, and
contains his jade death mask within.

The temple, which had the ancient name of Lakamha,
meaning Big Water, has five plain, rectangular entrances,
and rises to 35 metres (115 feet) in height. Six panels flank
the entrances and are covered in images and hieroglyphs
that include symbols of Palenque's main gods and Pakal's
son and his mother, Sak K'uk' (r.612–15 CE). The temple's
vaulted roof features a comb decoration that is typical of
Palenque architecture. The interior walls are also covered
with carved inscriptions, hence the temple's name. When
first built, it was covered in a thick layer of brightly
coloured stucco.

MAYAN ARCHITECTS
The Maya lived in Central
America, including southern
Mexico and Guatemala, and
Mayan architects took inspiration from earlier Mesoamerican
cultures, especially the
Olmecs and Teotihuacan. They
used local materials such as
limestone, sandstone and
volcanic tuff, cutting blocks of
stone with stone tools. Mud and
burnt-lime cement were used
to create forms of concrete.

DOME **p.172** ARCH **p.173** STAIRCASE **p.176** COLUMN **p.177** PORTICO/PORCH **p.186** STONE **p.192**
BRICK **p.195**

Dome of the Rock

691 CE

RAJA IBN HAYWAH • YAZID IBN SALLAM: JERUSALEM

Other key works
Great Mosque of Mecca, architect unknown, 692 CE, Hejaz, Saudi Arabia
Imam Husayn Shrine, architect unknown, 684 CE, Karbala, Iraq
Imam Reza Shrine, architect unknown, 818 CE, Mashhad, Iran

Built on a site that is important to Jews, Christians and Muslims, the Dome of the Rock is also known as Qubbat al-Sakhrah in Arabic and Kippat ha-Sela in Hebrew.

Constructed over the rock from which the prophet Mohammed is said to have ascended to heaven, where Abraham offered his son Isaac to God, and that was once the site of the Temple of Solomon, the Dome of the Rock follows Syrian Byzantine designs. Rising from a drum supported by a circular arcade of four piers and twelve columns taken from ancient Roman sites, its gold dome is almost 35 metres (115 feet) in height and 20 metres (66 feet) in diameter. It was originally solid gold, later replaced with copper and then aluminium, and it is now aluminium coated with gold leaf.

Initially commissioned by the Umayyad Caliph Abd al-Malik (646–705 CE), the octagonal building follows the proportions and design of the nearby Church of the Holy Sepulchre (335 CE), and features blue and gold tiles imported from Turkey. In Islamic art, blue represents the sky, suggesting infinity, while gold represents the knowledge of God. The dome shape symbolizes Mohammed's ascent to heaven, as well as the wholeness and balance of the Muslim faith, while both the dome and the exterior walls include many windows, allowing light to flood in. Inside, two concentric ambulatories or walkways, one circular and one octagonal, are formed by colonnades.

RAJA IBN HAYWAH AND YAZID IBN SALLAM
Not much is known about the architects of the Dome of the Rock. It is probable that they were Raja ibn Haywah (d.730 CE), and Yazid ibn Sallam (dates unknown). Between 687 and 691 CE, the Umayyad Caliph Abd al-Malik ibn Marwan (r.685–705 CE) instructed the two men to construct a dome with 'the best materials available to them'.

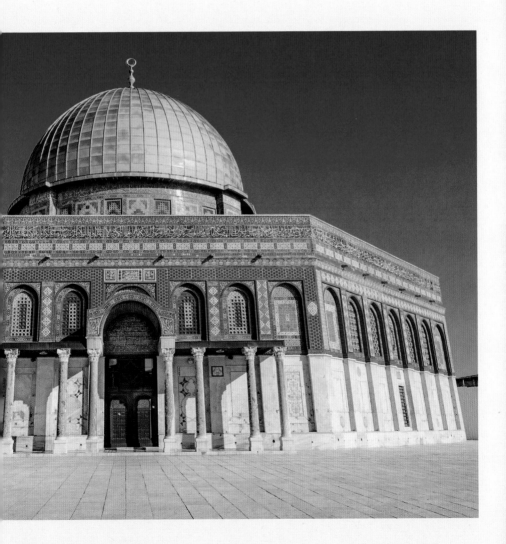

DOME **p.172**   ARCH **p.173**   COLUMN **p.177**   STONE **p.192**   BRICK **p.195**   TILES **p.198**   MARBLE **p.200**
MOSAIC **p.204**   GLASS **p.206**

Prambanan

855 CE

JAVA, INDONESIA

A ninth-century temple complex in Indonesia on the borders of Yogyakarta and Central Java, Prambanan was probably built to mark the return of the Hindu Sanjaya dynasty to power in Central Java.

After nearly a century of Buddhist dominance, King Rakai Pikatan (r.838–50 CE) commissioned a temple to honour Lord Shiva. Subsequent rulers expanded it, resulting in a compound of three zones. The outer zone was a large open space, the middle zone contained over 200 small, identical shrines, while the holiest inner zone contained the main temples and more small shrines surrounded by a square stone wall with a gate at each of the four cardinal points. In the centre of the inner shrine are three *Trimurti* temples dedicated to the three forms of divinity, personified as Shiva (the Transformer), Brahma (the Creator) and Vishnu (the Preserver).

Measuring 47 metres (154 feet) tall and 34 metres (111½ feet) wide, the Shiva Temple is the tallest and largest structure in the complex, designed to a cruciform plan on a square base with four formal staircases. All the shrines in the central and middle zones are intricately carved with reliefs relaying stories from the Indonesian version of the Ramayana epic. The entire complex conforms to traditional Hindu temple design in following a geometric grid that is dominated by the central building. Because much of the building material was organic, many original structures no longer remain.

HINDU **p.19**

Other key works

Kanchi Kailasanathar Temple, architect unknown, 685–705 CE, Kanchipuram, India

Brihadeeswarar Temple, architect unknown, 1000–10, Thanjavur, India

Kandariya Mahadeva Temple, architect unknown, c.1005–30, Khajuraho, India

HINDU ARCHITECTS

The earliest Hindu architects created simple rock-cut cave shrines, but later massive, ornate temples were produced. Based on grid ground plans with square forms, soaring towers and elaborate decorative sculpture, these were considered the dwelling places of certain gods. Early materials used were wood and terracotta, but architects gradually moved on to brick, stone and especially marble.

TOWER **p.174** STAIRCASE **p.176** SPIRE **p.184** STONE **p.192** BRICK **p.195**

Maria Laach Abbey

1093
–
1230

ANDERNACH, GERMANY

Other key works

Notre Dame La Grande, architect unknown, 1086–1150, Poitiers, France

Santiago de Compostela, Maestro Esteban, Bernard the Elder, Robertus Galperinus and Bernard the Younger, 1075–1211, Santiago de Compostela, Spain

Speyer Cathedral, architect unknown, 1030–61, Speyer, Germany

ROMANESQUE ARCHITECTS
Apart from the Italian Benedetto Antelami (c.1150–1230) and the Spanish Master Mateo (c.1150–c.1200), few Romanesque architects' names are known but, like these two, many were also sculptors. They used their understanding of mass, scale and negative space to exper- iment, while also overseeing teams of quarrymen, builders and decorators. Churchmen were usually in charge of the financial administration.

One of the tallest German Romanesque churches, Maria Laach Abbey stands on the south-western shore of a large volcanic lake, the Laacher See.

Founded in 1093 by the Count Palatine of the Rhine, Heinrich II (d.1095) and his wife Adelheid (d.1100), this massive Benedictine Abbey was mainly built with local lava by master builders from Lombardy. The crypt and some exterior walls had been completed by the time of Heinrich's death, but when Adelheid died five years later, construction stopped. Building resumed in 1152, and the crypt, timber-roofed nave and western choir were consecrated in 1156 by the Archbishop of Trier, Hillin of Falmagne (c.1100–69).

Each end of the imposing abbey features three towers. The largest square tower stands at the west end, its helm roof forming a diamond shape, and it is flanked by two round towers with triangular-shaped roof sections. The west porch was constructed between 1220 and 1230 by master builders from Burgundy, who gave it a large atrium and may also have replaced the flat timber roof of the abbey's nave with a stone vault. The rounded exterior arcade on the outside of the colonnaded porch is echoed by the rounded arches inside. The grand westwork (an entrance area at the west end of a church) conforms to the German Romanesque style in being broader than the width of the nave and aisles. Later, under Abbot Diedrich II von Lehmen (1256–95), some Gothic additions were made.

ROMANESQUE **p.24**

TOWER **p.174** COURTYARD **p.175** COLUMN **p.177** ATRIUM **p.180** VAULT **p.183** STONE **p.192**
BRICK **p.195** PLASTER **p.203** GLASS **p.206**

Angkor Wat

SIEM REAP, CAMBODIA

C.1113
—
C.1150

In continuous use since it was built in the twelfth
century, the west-facing Angkor Wat temple complex was
originally dedicated to the Hindu god Vishnu, but was
later converted to Buddhist use.

Soon after becoming king of the Khmer Empire,
Suryavarman II (r.1113–50) commissioned Angkor Wat.
It was designed as a pyramid representing the structure of
the universe: the centre of the temple represented Mount
Meru, the home of the Hindu gods, with the five towers
rising on a series of colonnaded platforms representing
the five peaks of the mountain. These towers are behind

arcaded walls at different levels, with a long causeway leading from the western gateway of the outer wall to the main temple precinct. The wide rectangular moat around the complex represented the mythical oceans surrounding the earth. Two small stone shrines adjoin the causeway near the centre.

The temple itself has covered galleries on all sides that contain gateways indicating the route to the central shrine, while the climb to the central shrine echoes the ascent to a real mountain peak. Nearly 2,000 square metres (21,000 square feet) of bas-reliefs adorn the walls, with carved lintels, friezes and pediments depicting the Hindu epics Ramayana and Mahabharata. Most of Angkor Wat is built of sandstone and laterite, a local clay that hardens rapidly when exposed to the sun and air.

KHMER ARCHITECTURE
Known for its abundance of carvings, sculpture and reliefs, Khmer architecture flourished from approximately the early 9th century to the first half of the 15th. Khmer architects adhered to strict religious and political ideas, originally imported from India but adapted to local conditions, such as Angkor Wat's galleried temple on its terrace.

Other key works
Pre Rup Temple, architect unknown, 961 CE, Siem Reap, Cambodia
Banteay Srei Temple, architect unknown, 967 CE, Siem Reap, Cambodia
Ta Prohm, architect unknown, 1186, Siem Reap, Cambodia

TERRACE **p.187** STONE **p.192** BRICK **p.195**

Krak des Chevaliers

HOMS, SYRIA

1142
–
1171

THE KNIGHTS HOSPITALLERS
During the Crusades, from 1096 to 1272, the design of castles in
Europe became heavily influenced by Islamic architecture. Just before
the start of the Crusades, the Hospitaller Order formed to care for sick,
poor or injured pilgrims in the Holy Land. Once the Crusades began,
they became military monks and built various fortifications as their
headquarters abroad.

GOTHIC **p.25**

Other key works
Margat Castle, architect unknown, 1062, Baniyas, Syria
Caerphilly Castle, architect unknown, 1268–90, Caerphilly, UK
Beaumaris Castle, James of St George, 1295–1330, Anglesey, UK

Dominating the surrounding land, the Krak des Chevaliers is classified as both a spur castle, thanks to its position on top of a 650 metre (2,100 foot) high hill, and a concentric castle, thanks to its curtain walls.

Originally, the castle was called Le Crat by the Franks, but after a while its name became confused with *karak*, the Syriac word for fortress. Built by the Hospitaller Order of Saint John of Jerusalem during the Crusades, the castle was in a strategically important location, 40 kilometres (25 miles) from the city of Homs, on the route from Antioch to Beirut and the Mediterranean Sea. It was used by the Hospitallers as their base in the Middle East for decades, and the architecture combines European Gothic features with medieval and Islamic military elements. Gothic features include high ceilings and towers, tracery and delicate decoration, and pointed arches on doors and windows. Thirteenth-century additions included machicolations – openings between the corbels supporting the battlements – inspired by Muslim architecture.

Made predominantly with limestone, the inner castle was defended by a curtain wall incorporating seven towers, each 10 metres (33 feet) in diameter. Some parts of this protective wall were over three metres (10 feet) thick. Within was a courtyard surrounded by vaulted chambers, with huge storerooms and vast stables that could be filled with provisions and horses, enabling the inhabitants to protect and support themselves if necessary.

ROOF **p.168** TOWER **p.174** COURTYARD **p.175** STAIRCASE **p.176** ATRIUM **p.180**
VAULT **p.183** STONE **p.192** BRICK **p.195** PLASTER **p.203**

Chartres Cathedral

1194
—
1250

CHARTRES, FRANCE

Other key works

Notre Dame, architect unknown, c.1163–1345, Paris, France

Beauvais Cathedral, Jean d'Orbais, Jean-Le-Loup, Gaucher de Reims and Bernard de Soissons, 1225–1573, Beauvais, France

Salisbury Cathedral, Elias de Dereham, 1220–58, Wiltshire, UK

South-west of Paris, Chartres Cathedral was the fifth cathedral to be built on a site that had been revered by both druids and Romans, and the first of several High Gothic cathedrals built from the end of the twelfth century on.

As famous for its stained glass as for its architecture, Chartres Cathedral has a soaring 34 metre (111½ feet) high vault, and contains 3,000 square metres (32,300 square feet) of stained glass. After a previous cathedral had been destroyed by fire in 1194, architects designed the new one in a cruciform plan with a main building roughly 130 metres (430 feet) in length. Among its features are a nave arcade, ambulatory and radiating chapels, an arcaded triforium gallery, large clerestory windows, lancet windows, an oculus window and jewel-like rose windows. The extraordinary height was made possible through its heavy flying buttresses and supporting piers, which also allowed the walls to support the huge stained-glass windows.

Chartres Cathedral took just 26 years to complete, with the north and south transept porches finished later, between 1224 and 1250. The enormous nave includes porches adorned with sculpture and reliefs of biblical scenes. At the west end are two mismatched spires: a 105 metre (349 foot) pyramid-style structure built in c.1160, and its 113 metre (371 foot) companion built in the Flamboyant style during the sixteenth century.

GOTHIC ARCHITECTS

With most of their work coming from the Church, Gothic architects designed abbeys and cathedrals that appeared light and airy, inspiring all who saw or entered them to feel closer to God. They frequently included huge, colourful stained-glass windows. Spires, flying buttresses and pointed arches were both structural and decorative, while vaulted ceilings opened up the interior spaces.

ARCH **p.173** COLUMN **p.177** BUTTRESS **p.178** VAULT **p.183** SPIRE **p.184** PORTICO/PORCH **p.186**
STONE **p.192** BRICK **p.195** GLASS **p.206**

Alhambra

GRANADA, SPAIN

1238
–
1358

Other key works
Alcázar, architect unknown,
913–1366, Seville, Spain
Moorish Castle, architect
unknown, 14th century, Gibraltar
Generalife, architect unknown,
fourteenth century, Granada, Spain

From the Arabic *al hamra*, meaning red house, the Alhambra is an ancient mosque, palace and fortress complex, built towards the end of the medieval period.

Including royal residential quarters, court rooms, official chambers and a mosque, most of the architecture that survives today was constructed for the Nasrid dynasty (1230–1492), the last Islamic sultanate in Spain. Moorish poets described the Alhambra as a 'pearl set in emeralds'. Laid out as an independent fortified town surrounding by a wall, it contains approximately thirty towers and four large gateways, and was used as both the

ISLAMIC **p.20** MOORISH **p.22**

Islamic seat of government and the sultan's residence. Extending over an area of about 10.5 hectares (26 acres), it comprised three independent sectors. One sector was a citadel where a military force was stationed; another was the palace where the sultan and his family lived and the court gathered; and another was the Medina, a small town for court and administrative officials.

Among the architectural features of the Alhambra is the Court of Lions, with its large fountain flanked by twelve marble lions, from which water flows in the four cardinal directions. The nearby Court of the Myrtles has a long pool framed by finely columned arcades, and leads to the Hall of the Ambassadors, which features a vaulted wooden ceiling inlaid with seven tiers of star-shaped patterns, suggesting the seven heavens in the Qu'ran.

MOORISH ARCHITECTS
Built under the rule of the Nasrids, the last Arab-Muslim dynasty in Spain, the Alhambra adhered to Islamic conventions as much as possible on such a rocky site. The architects' names have been lost, but the series of courtyards, with slender-columned arcades, fountains and water basins, was created to represent paradise as it was described in Islamic poetry.

ARCH **p.173** COLUMN **p.177** TERRACE **p.187** STONE **p.192** BRICK **p.195** GLASS **p.206**

Santa Maria del Fiore

1294
–
1436

ARNOLFO DI CAMBIO • FILIPPO BRUNELLESCHI
FRANCESCO TALENTI • GIOVANNI DI LAPO GHINI • ALBERTO ARNOLDI
GIOVANNI D'AMBROGIO • NERI DI FIORAVANTE • ANDREA ORCAGNA:
FLORENCE, ITALY

Other key works
Ospedale degli Innocenti, Filippo
Brunelleschi, 1445, Florence, Italy
San Lorenzo, Filippo Brunelleschi,
1422–70, Florence, Italy
Palazzo Medici-Riccardi,
Michelozzo di Bartolomeo
Michelozzi, 1459, Florence, Italy

Although predominantly Gothic in design, Santa Maria del Fiore reflects many Renaissance achievements.

In 1294, Florence's city council commissioned Arnolfo di Cambio (1240–1310) 'to make a design ... in a style of magnificence which neither the industry, not the power of man can surpass'. He designed a massive vaulted basilica with an octagonal crossing, but could not engineer a dome large enough to cover the space. With modifications, construction of the cathedral continued for over a century. Then in 1418, Filippo Brunelleschi (1377–1446) won a competition for a viable dome and work continued for many years thereafter. Using an

Right: Giotto's Campanile was built from 1334 to 1359. At 84 m (275 ft) in height, it was extremely tall for the time, but Giotto intended to make it even taller with a spire. However, he died in 1337, and the spire was abandoned.

ARNOLFO DI CAMBIO AND FILIPPO BRUNELLESCHI
Initially sought after as a painter and sculptor, Arnolfo di Cambio worked as an architect in Rome from 1266 and in Florence from 1294. Similarly, Brunelleschi began as a goldsmith and sculptor, but from the age of 23 his architectural commissions increasingly took over. Inspired by ancient Roman proportion and structure, his work exemplifies the transition between Gothic and Renaissance styles.

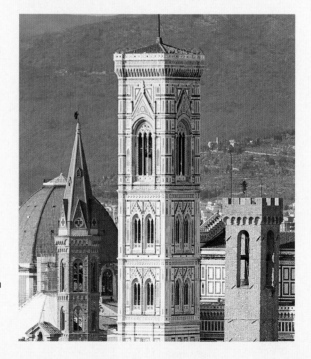

Left: The masonry of the dome consists of brickwork in a herringbone pattern, held between several stone ribs. The lantern at the top of the dome was completed in 1461 after Brunelleschi had died.

Below: Coloured marble, mainly green and white, was used on the Cathedral's façades in patterns, including vertical and horizontal bands and curves. Three apses were built at the eastern end of the Cathedral with half-domed roofs.

ancient Roman technique that had been employed in the Pantheon (see page 60), his dome was double-skinned, self-supporting and made of brick. The strong herringbone-patterned inner shell supported the lighter outer one, and no scaffolding was needed to erect it. Rising to 91 metres (300 feet), it is the largest brick dome ever constructed.

The entire cathedral complex consists of three buildings: the Cathedral, the Baptistery and the Campanile, or bell tower. Forming a Latin cross, the Cathedral has a wide central nave comprising four square bays, with an aisle on two sides. Over the centuries, numerous other architects worked on the project, including contributions from Giotto di Bondone (c.1267–1337) and Andrea Pisano (1290–1348) on the Campanile. Francesco Talenti (1300–70) finally completed the Campanile in 1359 and enlarged the octagon under the dome eight years later, preparing the way for Brunelleschi's masterpiece. For centuries, Santa Maria del Fiore was the largest church in Europe.

DOME **p.172** ARCH **p.173** COLUMN **p.177** STONE **p.192** BRICK **p.195** STAINED GLASS **p.207**

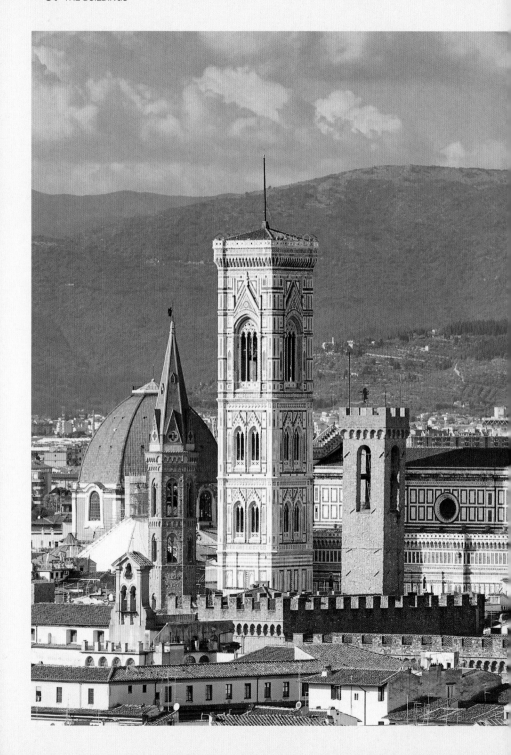

Doge's Palace

FILIPPO CALENDARIO • ANTONIO RIZZO • ANTONIO DA PONTE
ANDREA PALLADIO: VENICE, ITALY

1340
–
1580

A prominent landmark of the city of Venice, the Doge's Palace was the residence of the city state's elected leader, the Doge, who acted as the supreme authority of the Venetian Republic.

Overlooking the Piazza San Marco, the Doge's Palace remained the seat of power for 700 years. Within it were law courts, administrative offices, courtyards, ballrooms, ceremonial staircases and prisons. Built predominantly in the Venetian Gothic style with Byzantine elements and Renaissance and Mannerist additions, the palace comprises three large blocks, patterned with pink Verona marble and white Istrian stone.

The construction of the earliest part, the Venetian Gothic façade that faces the water, began in 1340. Its gallery was inspired by Byzantine models, consisting of a line of columns that are thinner and spaced more closely than the columns on the ground floor. These support delicate-looking tracery formed by ogee (double-curve) and trefoil (three-lobe) arches, which carry quatrefoil (four-lobe) openings within roundels. The large expanse of wall above the two open storeys gives the palace a top-heavy appearance, so the patterning of marble in soft colours was applied to create a lightening effect. Over the centuries, numerous expansions occurred, including after 1574 and 1577, when two fires ravaged parts of the building. In the late sixteenth century, additional prison cells were erected in a separate building, the Prigioni Nuove (New Prisons), across the canal, connected to the palace via the Bridge of Sighs.

THE ARCHITECTS OF THE DOGE'S PALACE
Records are unclear, but several architects worked on the Doge's Palace. Filippo Calendario (c.1315–55) may have designed much of the original building. After the 1574 fire, the head architect was Antonio da Ponte (1512–97), whose nephew Antonio Contino (dates unknown) designed the Bridge of Sighs in 1600. Also after the fire, Andrea Palladio contributed interiors, fortifications and decorations.

GOTHIC **p.25** RENAISSANCE **p.26** PALLADIAN **p.28**

Other key works
Santa Maria Gloriosa dei Frari, Jacopo Celega, 1250–1338, Venice, Italy
Ca d'Oro, Bartolomeo Bon and Giovanni Bon, 1428–30, Venice, Italy
Palazzo Cavalli-Franchetti, architect unknown, 1565, Venice, Italy

ARCH **p.173** COLUMN **p.177** TERRACE **p.187** STONE **p.192** BRICK **p.195** GLASS **p.206**

Temple of the Sun

MACHU PICCHU, PERU

C.1450

INCA ARCHITECTURE

Inca buildings were uniform in design and specifically incorporated the natural landscape in their design, blending geometrical and natural forms. Stone was the main material, finely worked into interlocking polished blocks. These heavy blocks were moved using ropes, logs, poles, levers and ramps. Once on site, they were cut so precisely that mortar was not necessary.

Situated on a mountain ridge 2,430 metres (7,970 feet) above sea level is a fifteenth-century Inca citadel known as Machu Picchu.

With its polished dry-stone walls, Machu Picchu was built in the classical Inca style. Among its most prominent structures are the Intihuatana stone (often translated as the 'hitching post of the sun'), the Room of the Three Windows and the Temple of the Sun. As the Incas believed that they were descended from the sun god Inti, their beliefs and rituals were connected to the sun and to the rest of the cosmos.

Built on granite rock, the Temple of the Sun is constructed with stones that were shaped and polished so that they fitted tightly together. The building forms a semi-circular shape with a tower rising from it that contains a trapezoid-shaped window. In the centre of the temple is a large rock that was almost certainly an altar, and beneath is a cave that was probably the burial place of the Inca ruler Pachacutec (r.1438–71), who had Machu Picchu constructed. Along the back wall of the temple are several small holes that are commonly believed to have been studded with small coloured gemstones, and the entire structure was positioned so that during the summer and winter solstices, the rising sun shone directly through certain windows.

Other key works
Sacsayhuamán, architect unknown, c.13th century, Cusco, Peru
Watchtower, architect unknown, c.1450, Ollantaytambo, Peru
Coricancha (originally Inti Kancha), architect unknown, c.1450, Cusco, Peru

WINDOW **p.167** TOWER **p.174** COURTYARD **p.175** STONE **p.192**

Saint Peter's Basilica

1506 – 1615

DONATO BRAMANTE • BALDASSARE PERUZZI • CARLO MADERNO
ANTONIO DA SANGALLO • MICHELANGELO BUONARROTI • RAPHAEL:
ROME, ITALY

MICHELANGELO BUONARROTI
Widely admired across Europe as a sculptor and painter, Michelangelo was revered as an architect during his later years. For his work on Saint Peter's, he refused to take payment, declaring that it was his masterpiece. For Brunelleschi's Church of San Lorenzo in Florence, he designed the Medici Chapel and the tombs of Giuliano and Lorenzo de Medici.

Venerated since the first century as the burial site of Saint Peter, the Papal Basilica of Saint Peter's is the largest church in the world.

In 1506, Bramante (1444–1514) was commissioned by Pope Julius II (1443–1513) to design a new church for the site. Inspired by the Pantheon (see page 60), he proposed a huge Greek cross with a dome covering Saint Peter's shrine. After Bramante died, Raphael (1483–1520) took over the design and construction, and after his death, several other architects, including Baldassare Peruzzi (1481–1536) and Antonio da Sangallo the Younger (1484–1546) continued. Eventually, at the age of 72, Michelangelo (1475–1564) took on the project.

Upholding much of Bramante's plan, including the centralized Greek-cross format that others had abandoned, Michelangelo created a stronger, more dynamic and unified design, replacing single columns with pairs, and adding a massive dome measuring 136.5 metres (448 feet) in height. After his death, further architects including Giacomo della Porta (1532–1602) followed Michelangelo's plans closely. In 1606, Carlo Maderno (1556–1629) added a short nave with a high façade and a projecting portico, with Corinthian columns and second-floor windows for papal speeches. The whole building is as high as it is wide, and the dome is created from a single shell of concrete, mixed with volcanic tuff and pumice for lightness. At the summit is an ocular opening, eight metres (26 feet) across that bathes the interior with light.

Other key works
Santa Maria di Montesanto and Santa Maria dei Miracoli, Carlo Rinaldi, Carlo Fontana and Gian Lorenzo Bernini, 1662–77, Rome, Italy
Basilica of Superga, Filippo Juvarra, 1717–31, Turin, Italy
Les Invalides, Jules Hardouin-Mansart, 1675–1706, Paris, France

RENAISSANCE **p.26** BAROQUE **p.29**

DOME **p.172** COLUMN **p.177** PORTICO/PORCH **p.186** STONE **p.192** BRICK **p.195** CONCRETE **p.201**
GLASS **p.206**

Shibam

HADHRAMAUT, YEMEN

1540
–
1600

Other key works

Chan Chan, architect unknown, c.850–1470 CE, Trujillo, Peru

Arg-e Bam, architect unknown, 579–323 BCE, Bam, Iran

Birni, architect unknown, c.1050 CE, Zinder, Niger

ISLAMIC **p.20**

Deep in a remote valley of Yemen, in the desert of Ramlat al-Sab'atayn, is the city of Shibam, often called Shibam Hadhramaut because of its role as a trading post and then, from the third century CE, as capital of the Kingdom of Hadhramaut.

Surrounded by a seven metre (23 feet) fortified wall, Shibam is built on a rocky spur to give inhabitants a vantage point and protect it from flooding. The city was largely rebuilt after one such flood in 1532–3, and is an outstanding example of traditional Hadrami architecture, arranged on a rectangular grid. Comprising approximately 500 tower-block houses of between six and ten storeys, some rising to about 30.5 metres (100 feet) in height, it has been nicknamed both 'the Manhattan of the desert' and 'the Chicago of the desert'. The height of these towers was in part a means of protection, but also a signal of a family's economic or political prestige.

The buildings are all constructed from bricks made out of local fertile soil mixed with hay and water, then shaped and dried in the sun rather than fired. The towers are then whitewashed with a layer of protective limestone or crushed gypsum to render them water-resistant. The tallest are built on stone foundations and their windowless ground floors were originally used for livestock and grain storage, while the upper levels had one or two rooms on each floor to house families.

MUD-BRICK ARCHITECTURE
The majority of houses in ancient Africa, Europe, Asia and the Americas were built with mud-bricks, which were cheap, easy to make and practical. Although it is rarely discussed, mud-brick architecture was more common than stone architecture in ancient Egypt, with buildings and structures made from unfired mud-bricks standing alongside stone tombs and temples.

→ ROOF **p.168** ARCH **p.173** TOWER **p.174** STAIRCASE **p.176** STONE **p.192** MUD-BRICK/ADOBE **p.193**

Saint Basil's Cathedral

BARMA • POSTNIK YAKOVLEV: MOSCOW, RUSSIA

1555
–
1561

Other key works
Cathedral of Santa Sophia,
architect unknown, 1045–52,
Novgorod, Russia
Church of the Transfiguration,
architect unknown, 1714, Kizhi,
Russia
Alexander Nevsky Cathedral,
Alexander Pomerantsev,
1894–1912, Tallinn, Estonia

The Cathedral of the Protection of Most Holy Theotokos on the Moat, also known as the Cathedral of Vasily the Blessed, or Saint Basil's Cathedral, is a former church in Red Square in Moscow.

Commemorating the defeat of the Mongols at the battle of Kazan in 1552, Saint Basil's comprises eight small side chapels arranged around a central church, forming a star-like pattern that follows the shape of New Jerusalem as described in the Book of Revelation. A further chapel was erected in 1588 over the grave of the local saint Vasily, or Basil.

Commissioned by Ivan IV (1530–84), known as Ivan the Terrible, each chapel has a tower and an onion-shaped dome, individually decorated, and linked by narrow, winding passages. Built on the four cardinal points of the compass, the four larger chapels stand on massive foundations, while the four smaller chapels are on raised platforms, symbolizing their position between heaven and earth. They and the central chapel are octagonal, while the four diagonally placed smaller chapels are cuboid. Although the cathedral looks symmetrical from the outside, the building was carefully planned with its domes at different heights. The entire structure was built in brick on a timber frame, and the bright colours were added between the 1680s and 1848. Based on the dome of the grand mosque in Kazan, which had been destroyed by Ivan in 1552, onion-shaped domes soon became the fashion for all Russian Orthodox churches.

BARMA AND POSTNIK YAKOVLEV
It is possible that the 16th-century architect Postnik Yakovlev and Barma (dates unknown) were the same person. Barma may have been a nickname, or he may have been Postnik's brother or his assistant. Most famous for Saint Basil's, Postnik created a building with no precedent, yet which influenced all subsequent Russian Orthodox cathedral architecture.

BYZANTINE **p.17** RENAISSANCE **p.26**

DOME **p.172**   TOWER **p.174**   COLUMN **p.177**   BRICK **p.195**   WOOD **p.196**   GLASS **p.206**

Villa La Rotonda

ANDREA PALLADIO: VICENZA, ITALY

1567
—
C.1592

Villa Almerico Capra, better known as La Rotonda, is a Renaissance villa in northern Italy, built for a retired priest from the Vatican, Paolo Almerico (1514–89).

With echoes of the dome of the Pantheon in Rome (see page 60), La Rotonda was designed by Andrea Palladio (1508–80) as a square, symmetrical building with each of the four façades having a projecting portico. Each of these four porticos has a pediment adorned with statues of classical deities and supported by six ionic columns. The name La Rotonda refers to the central circular hall and dome. To ensure that each room in the villa received some sunlight, the design was rotated 45 degrees from the cardinal points of the compass.

Building began in 1567, but neither Palladio nor Almerico saw the villa's completion. After Palladio's death, a second architect, Vincenzo Scamozzi (1548–1616), was employed by the new owners, and one of the major changes he made to the original plan was to modify the two-storey central hall. Palladio had intended it to be covered by a high semi-circular dome but Scamozzi designed a shallower dome with an oculus open to the sky. In the end, his dome was completed with a cupola. All rooms were proportioned with mathematical precision according to Palladio's personal rules of architecture, published in his 1570 book *I Quattro Libri dell'Architettura* (*The Four Books of Architecture*). The central, circular hall with its soaring domed ceiling is covered by frescoes, creating a cathedral-like atmosphere.

Other key works
Villa Cornaro, Andrea Palladio, 1553–4, Piombino Dese, Italy
Villa Foscari, Andrea Palladio, 1558–60, Venice, Italy
Villa Valmarana, Andrea Palladio, 1542, Vicenza, Italy

RENAISSANCE **p.26** PALLADIAN **p.28**

ANDREA PALLADIO
Born in Padua, Italy, in 1508, Andrea Palladio initially worked as a stonemason,
then studied architecture. In 1549, Palladio won a competition to remodel an early
Renaissance palace in Vicenza. It was a great success, and for the next 30 years, he
designed many more palaces, churches and villas in Italy, drawing largely on his study
of ancient Roman architecture.

DOME **p.172** COLUMN **p.177** PORTICO/PORCH **p.186** STONE **p.192** BRICK **p.195** GLASS **p.206**
STUCCO **p.205**

Taj Mahal

USTAD AHMAD LAHORI: AGRA, INDIA

1632
–
1648

Commissioned by the Mughal emperor Shah Jahan (1592–1666) for his favourite wife, Mumtaz Mahal (1593–1631), the Taj Mahal was created as a mausoleum, or monument of 'undying love'.

Expanding upon traditions of both Persian and Mughal architecture, the Taj Mahal is also inspired by earlier mausoleums, including the Gur-e Amir (1403–04) in Samarkand and Humayun's Tomb (1565–71) in Delhi, but it is quite unique. Following a complex plan, it has a large central octagonal hall on a square plinth, topped by a huge onion-shaped dome with a finial that blends Islamic and Hindu motifs. The main dome is echoed by smaller domes on detached, ornamental minarets, while slender, octagonal pinnacles topped with lotus-petal shapes are attached to the corners of the building.

Spreading across a vast 170,000 square metres (42 acres), the Taj Mahal is made predominantly with white marble inlaid with semi-precious stones. At the centre of each façade is an *iwan* (arched portal), and there is a *chhatri* (small domed pavilion on slim pillars) on either side of the central hall. All elements of the building feature carved and inlaid decorations, mainly of plants and flowers, while the entire structure is reflected in a long water channel that stretches directly from the north façade towards the main gateway. Using geometry and symmetry, each side of the Taj Mahal is identical so that no matter which direction it is approached from, it always looks the same.

USTAD AHMAD LAHORI
Although the architect of the Taj Mahal is not confirmed, it is likely that the chief designer was the Persian Ustad Ahmad Lahori (1580–1649). Approximately 22,000 labourers worked on the construction. To protect it from potential earthquake damage, its four minarets slant slightly away. Its timber foundations are kept strong and moist by the Yamuna River.

MUGHAL **p.27**

Other key works

Gur-e Amir, architect unknown, 1403–04, Samarkand, Uzbekistan

Humayun's Tomb, Mirak Mirza Ghiyas and Sayyid Muhammad, 1565–71, Delhi, India

Masjid-i Imam, Badi' al-Zaman Tuni and Ali Akbar al-Isfahani, 1611–38, Isfahan, Iran

DOME **p.172** ARCH **p.173** MINARET **p.185** PORTICO/PORCH **p.186** STONE **p.192** BRICK **p.195** WOOD **p.196** MARBLE **p.200** STUCCO **p.205**

Rinshunkaku

1649

YOKOHAMA, JAPAN

Other key works
Katsura Imperial Villa, architect unknown, 17th century, Kyoto, Japan
Kamiyashiki of Matsudaira Tadamasa, architect unknown, 17th century, Tokyo, Japan
Shugakuin Imperial Villa, architect unknown, 1659, Kyoto, Japan

Built during the early Edo Period (1603–1867), this villa was the summer residence of Tokugawa Yorinobu, the first feudal lord of the Kishu Tokugawa clan.

The villa originally stood in Iwade, in Wakayama on the Kinokawa River, but in 1915 the building was moved to the Sankei-en gardens in Yokohama and named Rinshunkaku. It is constructed in the Sukiya architectural style, which developed at the end of the sixteenth century and continued until the nineteenth, originally for tea houses, but later also for private residences. Rinshunkaku is divided into three sections, including two single-storey structures with cypress-bark

JAPANESE **p.18**

SUKIYA ARCHITECTURE

During the Azuchi-Momoyama (1574–1600) and Tokugawa or Edo (1603–1867) periods, a style of architecture developed known as Sukiya style based on tea-house aesthetics. Buildings were created to appear as natural as possible, and to fit in calmly with their surroundings. Most architecture in this style had interior *fusumas* and an exterior *tsukimidai* (moon-viewing platform).

hip-and-gable roofs, and one two-storey structure with a cypress-bark rectangular hip roof and a shingled lower roof.

Overall, the design was intended to harmonize with its surroundings, with an emphasis on simplicity, using wood left as closely as possible in its natural state. Within the three buildings are twelve rooms, including the *hikae-no-ma* (a reception room for visitors); the *sekken-no-ma* (where the feudal lord greeted visitors); and the *okugata* (the private quarters of the feudal lord and his family). Inside on the *fusuma* (sliding interior panels) are ink paintings by prominent seventeenth-century artists of the Kano School. Transoms over the doors are decorated with sculpted waves in the first building, poetry-inscribed paper in the second building, and woodwind instruments in the third building.

→ WINDOW **p.167** ROOF **p.168** PORTICO/PORCH **p.186** WOOD **p.196** PAPER **p.197**

Palace of Versailles

c.1660 – 1715

LOUIS LE VAU • JULES HARDOUIN-MANSART: PARIS, FRANCE

Created for Louis XIV (1638–1715) by two of France's most celebrated architects, the Palace of Versailles is an outstanding example of French Baroque architecture.

Built around a former hunting lodge, the palace was designed primarily by Louis Le Vau (1612–70) and Jules Hardouin-Mansart (1646–1708). With two vast wings flanking a central block and courtyard, it was inhabited by the French monarch and the entire court from 1682 until the French Revolution in 1789. Le Vau designed the main building, and after 1678 Hardouin-Mansart extended it, adding the north and south wings and various state rooms. Particularly opulent features include the Hall of Mirrors with 17 tall windows each facing

LOUIS LE VAU AND JULES HARDOUIN-MANSART
Sought after for his innovative designs, Louis Le Vau was made first architect to the king in 1654, with projects including Vincennes Castle and La Salpêtrière Hospital. By the end of the 17th century, Jules Hardouin-Mansart was the most successful architect in France, and his work had a huge influence on Baroque architecture around the world.

Right: The original hunting lodge that stood on the site of Versailles was turned into a three-floor palace with a flat roof and wings. This black and white courtyard gave this part of the palace its name of the Marble Court.

BAROQUE **p.29** ROCOCO **p.30**

Other key works
Les Invalides, Jules Hardouin-
Mansart, 1706, Paris, France
Palais du Luxembourg, Salomon
de Brosse, 1615–20, Paris, France
Vaux-le-Vicomte, Louis Le Vau
and André Le Nôtre, 1656–61,
Maincy, France

Above: Alongside multicoloured
marbles, rich tapestries and expanses
of glass, Versailles made use of
ornate gilding on hundreds of door
and window frames, mouldings and
ornamental carvings. Its extravagance
came to symbolize the decadence and
absolutism of the monarchy,

Right: Every façade of Versailles is
different, and every one includes
numerous doors and French windows
in order to accommodate up to 3,000
people who lived there as part of the
French court. The masonry features
horizontal decorative bands.

an arched full-length mirror, marble pilasters, gilded
capitals and an ornately painted ceiling; the Marble
Court with gilding, pilasters, twin columns and elaborate
sculpture; the Royal Chapel, a two-storey structure with
a vaulted ceiling and apse, plus pilasters topped with
Corinthian capitals; and the Royal Opera, designed by
Ange-Jacques Gabriel (1698–1782), which can seat up to
1,200 guests, and is one of the earliest examples of what
would later become known as the Louis XVI style.

Set in extensive grounds, the palace, and in particular
its lavish interiors, revitalized architecture and design
across the world. These interiors, including furnishings,
upholstery and frescoes, were created by numerous
designers and artists, including Charles Le Brun
(1619–90), François Lemoyne (1688–1737) and Juste-
Aurèle Meissonier (1695–1750), while André Le Nôtre
(1613–1700) designed the gardens.

WINDOW **p.167** CHIMNEY **p.169** ARCH **p.173** COURTYARD **p.175** COLUMN **p.177** BRICK **p.195**
MARBLE **p.200** STUCCO **p.205** GLASS **p.206**

Saint Paul's Cathedral

CHRISTOPHER WREN: LONDON, UK

1675
–
1708

After the Great Fire of London, Christopher Wren (1632–1723) was commissioned to design over 50 new churches, among them a new cathedral for the site of Old Saint Paul's, which had been destroyed in the fire.

Wren's plans were approved in 1675, but significant construction did not begin until several years later – with modifications. Inspired by elements of Michelangelo's designs for Saint Peter's in Rome (see page 90), the new Saint Paul's included a dome measuring 111 metres (365 feet) in height, making it the tallest building in London until 1967. Composed of three shells – an inner shell, a concealed brick cone and an outer shell – the towering Baroque dome rests on pendentives between eight arches spanning the nave, choir, transepts and aisles. Around the drum beneath the dome is a continuous peristyle colonnade and an arrangement of alternating windows and projecting columns. Supporting the inner and outer domes, the peristyle is both decorative and practical. On either side of the dome area are wide transepts with semi-circular porticos.

The western front features a classical portico with paired columns on two storeys. Its twin bell towers are nearly 65 metres (213 feet) in height. Overall, the design incorporates elements of Gothic, Renaissance and classical styles, but predominantly adopts a restrained Baroque style, drawing on the architectural ideas of Inigo Jones (1573–1652) in England and Jules Hardouin-Mansart in France.

CHRISTOPHER WREN

Christopher Wren was a designer, astronomer, geometrician and founder (and president) of the Royal Society. He took up architecture when he was 30, and although his plan to rebuild the City of London after the Great Fire of 1666 never materialized, he designed many new buildings in the City and beyond, including the Royal Naval College, Greenwich, and numerous parish churches.

BAROQUE **p.29**

Other key works
Radcliffe Camera, James Gibbs, 1737–49, Oxford, UK
Saint Mary-Le-Bow, Christopher Wren, 1670–3, London, UK
Saint Martin, Ludgate, Christopher Wren, 1677–84, London, UK

WINDOW **p.167** DOME **p.172** ARCH **p.173** COLUMN **p.177** BRICK **p.195** MARBLE **p.200**
STUCCO **p.205** GLASS **p.206**

Wieskirche

DOMINIKUS ZIMMERMANN • JOHANN BAPTIST ZIMMERMANN:
BAVARIA, GERMANY

1745
–
1754

Other key works
Abbey Church, Egid Quirin Asam and Cosmas Damian Asam, 1724,
Kelheim, Germany
Rottenbuch Church, Joseph Schmuzer and Franz Xaver Schmuzer, 1747,
Rottenbuch, Germany
Saint John Nepomuk, Egid Quirin Asam and Cosmas Damian Asam, 1750,
Munich, Germany

BAROQUE **p.29** ROCOCO **p.30**

After real tears were apparently seen coming from a carved wooden statue of Christ near Steingaden, Bavaria in 1738, a pilgrimage church, the Wieskirche, sometimes known as the Meadow Church, was built at the site.

The new church had to be large because of the number of visitors. It also needed to be impressive, but not too ostentatious for its country surroundings. The resulting church is a blend of Rococo and Baroque expression. Local architects and artists, the brothers Dominikus (1685–1766) and Johann Baptist Zimmermann (1680–1758), designed an oval church that from the outside is unadorned, formed of straight lines. The interior however, is a light, airy structure. Eight piers support a grand entablature and vault, decorated with elaborately curving and gilded stucco and delicately coloured frescoes. To the east, a long, deep choir is surrounded by an upper and lower gallery.

Dominikus was in charge, and ensured that every aspect harmonized with the others, so for instance the trompe-l'œil paintings on the vaulted ceiling depict an iridescent blue sky with flying angels, contributing to the sense of exultation and exuberance. The main colours of the interior are gold, blue and red: gold symbolizes heaven, blue represents God's grace, and red connotes the blood of Christ. Coloured marble columns stand before long windows, and daylight floods into the building from these and other cleverly concealed and unexpected openings.

DOMINIKUS AND JOHANN BAPTIST ZIMMERMANN
Descending from a family of artists and craftsmen, Dominikus and Johann Baptist Zimmerman worked together. Initially, Dominikus was a stuccoist and later a master builder and architect. His elder brother Johann Baptist was a court stuccoist, fresco painter and architect, and the pair designed and executed almost every aspect of the construction and decoration of their buildings, most of them churches.

WINDOW **p.167** ROOF **p.168** COLUMN **p.177** MOULDING **p.181** NAVE **p.182** VAULT **p.183** PORTICO/PORCH **p.186** BRICK **p.195** MARBLE **p.200** STUCCO **p.205**

Hancock Shaker Village

1791
–
1961

MASSACHUSETTS, USA

Founded in the eighteenth century, the United Society of Believers in Christ's Second Appearing, or Shakers, built communal villages across America.

Hancock was the third of these villages to be established out of 19 founded in the United States between 1783 and 1836. During its peak, Hancock was home to over 300 Shakers. Family dwellings were built in the centre of the village, arranged in a linear plan as the basis of the close-knit community. These dwellings included communal rooms on the ground floor, separate entrances and stairs for males and females, and segregated bedrooms on the floors above. Other buildings in the village included the Meeting House (1793) and the Round Stone Barn (1826). All were large and spacious, deliberately devoid of decoration, and generally made of wood, granite, marble and other stone.

Shaker architects were banned from using decorative 'beadings, moulding and cornices', while elements such as door and window frames, lintels and chimneys were designed with plain and simple lines. Their religious laws stipulated that all meeting houses 'should be painted white without, and of a bluish shade within'. Hancock's original meeting house was built in 1786, with a large open room for religious dances, and was later enlarged and given a gable roof before being razed in 1938. The huge, unique Round Stone Barn reflected the importance of agriculture to the community.

SHAKER ARCHITECTURE
Shakers lived communally, and built environments for members to live, work and worship together. Shaker engineers levelled hillsides, redirected streams and built huge dwellings, offices, barns and meeting houses that featured such things as interior windows to carry natural light through rooms and double doorways and stairways for segregation. Their plain buildings were designed to outlast fashion.

SHAKER **p.33**

Other key works
Alfred Shaker Village, architects unknown, 1793–1931, Maine, USA
Canterbury Shaker Village, architects unknown, 1792–1992, New Hampshire, USA
Enfield Shaker Village, architects unknown, 1792–1917, Connecticut, USA

WINDOW **p.167** STAIRCASE **p.176** GABLE **p.179** STONE **p.192** BRICK **p.195** WOOD **p.196**

Capitol Building

1793
–
1863

WILLIAM THORNTON • THOMAS USTICK WALTER:
WASHINGTON, DC, USA

Other key works
The White House, James Hoban, 1792–1829, Washington, DC, USA
Virginia State Capitol, Thomas Jefferson, 1788, Richmond, USA
University of Virginia, Thomas Jefferson, 1822–6, Charlottesville, USA

The United States Congress formally began in March 1789, and passed an Act in July 1790 to establish a permanent capital city on a plot by the Potomac River, chosen by President George Washington (1732–99) as the site for the new capital city.

Washington asked the French engineer Pierre Charles L'Enfant (1754–1825) to design the new city. L'Enfant created an opulent plan, believing he would also design the principal structures, but was dismissed in 1792. Thomas Jefferson (1743–1826), who was then Secretary of State, felt that classical Graeco-Roman style architecture would best express the ideals of the new republic, and launched a competition for the Capitol's design in the same year. Amateur architect and physician William Thornton (1759–1828) won the contest with a Neoclassical entry with a central rotunda. For various reasons however, this design was later modified by the British-American architects Benjamin Henry Latrobe (1764–1820) and Charles Bulfinch (1763–1844).

In the 1850s, Pennsylvanian architect Thomas Ustick Walter (1804–87) expanded the north (Senate) and south (House of Representatives) wings on either side of the rotunda, and with the German-American architect August Schoenborn (1827–1902) designed a larger dome. At 29 metres (96 feet) in diameter, the rotunda rises 15 metres (48 feet) to the top of its walls and 54.9 metres (180 feet) to the canopy of the dome, which consists of inner and outer shells with an oculus at the top.

THOMAS USTICK WALTER
The fourth architect of the Capitol, Thomas Ustick Walter was responsible for extending the north and south wings and adding the central, cast-iron dome to the building. His plan more than doubled the size of the existing structure. The finished dome contains 108 windows and weighs 4,080 tonnes.

ROOF **p.168** DOME **p.172** COLUMN **p.177** PORTICO/PORCH **p.186** STONE **p.192** BRICK **p.195** STUCCO **p.205** GLASS **p.206**

Palace of Westminster

1840
–
1870

CHARLES BARRY • AUGUSTUS PUGIN: LONDON, UK

After a fire destroyed the original Palace of Westminster in 1834, a competition was held to design its replacement.

With aid from Augustus Pugin (1812–52), the experienced architect Charles Barry (1795–1860) won the commission. Influenced by fifteenth-century English churches, the vast building features a long, horizontal river façade of repeating windows dominated by vertical pinnacles, turrets and three large towers. Victoria Tower, the tallest and largest, rises over the Sovereign's Entrance, and is supported by an iron framework, concealed beneath a highly decorated stone façade with tall windows and statues in niches under ornate stone canopies. Above the Central Lobby, the octagonal Central Tower was built for ventilation. Featuring a spire, it contrasts visually with the other two towers. The Elizabeth Tower, commonly known as Big Ben, houses the Great Clock. Its four clock faces were designed by Pugin, as were the many pinnacles, finials and turrets rising from the building, each featuring ogees (double curves) and carved crockets (curved, leaf-like decorations).

Inside the Palace, a straight 'spine' of major rooms runs along the centre, including the Lords and Commons debating chambers and their separate lobbies, as well as the Central Lobby. Corridors lead off to parliamentary offices. The revival of Gothic elements influenced the design of many subsequent public buildings.

CHARLES BARRY AND AUGUSTUS PUGIN
A prolific architect, Charles Barry travelled widely and drew on architectural influences from countries such as France, Italy, Israel and Syria, particularly favouring classicism and Gothic designs. As a devout Catholic, Pugin particularly favoured the Gothic style. He was also fascinated by the Middle Ages, and he had a powerful influence on the Arts and Crafts movement.

GOTHIC REVIVAL **p.32** ←

Other key works
Highclere Castle, Charles Barry, 1839–42, Berkshire, UK
Dunrobin Castle, Charles Barry, 1835–50, Sutherland, UK
Nottingham Cathedral, Augustus Pugin, 1841–4, Nottinghamshire, UK

WINDOW **p.167** ROOF **p.168** TOWER **p.174** VAULT **p.183** SPIRE **p.184** STONE **p.192** GLASS **p.206** IRON **p.208**

Red House

1859 – 1860

PHILIP WEBB • WILLIAM MORRIS: KENT, UK

Co-designed by Philip Webb (1831–1915), who is often called the 'father of Arts and Crafts architecture', and the designer William Morris (1834–96), the Red House exemplifies the movement's ethos.

Morris decided to build a rural home for himself and his new wife Jane Morris (1839–1914), within commuting distance of central London, and employed his friend Webb to help him design and construct the house. Influenced by medievalism, Gothic Revival styles and his own ideas about craftsmanship, the Red House was one of the earliest examples of Arts and Crafts architecture. Designed to an unusual L-shaped plan, the red-brick building has two storeys and a high-pitched, red-tiled roof. The hall, dining room, library, morning room and kitchen are on the ground floor, with the main living rooms, drawing room, studio and bedrooms on the first floor.

Servants' quarters were larger and lighter than in most contemporary buildings, as Webb and Morris had strong ideas about working-class conditions. Windows were placed to suit the design of the rooms rather than to fit an external symmetry, so there are several different window types, including sash and round windows, tall casements and hipped dormers. There was no applied ornamentation and Morris and his friends designed and created almost everything inside, from furniture to tiles, candlesticks to tableware, and even stained-glass windows by Webb and Edward Burne-Jones (1833–98).

Other key works
Wightwick Manor, Edward Ould, 1887–93, Wolverhampton, UK
Derwent House, Ernest Newton 1899, Bromley, UK
Standen, Philip Webb, 1892–4, West Sussex, UK

WILLIAM MORRIS AND PHILIP WEBB

Architect, designer, writer, translator and socialist activist, William Morris was one of the most significant figures of the Arts and Crafts movement. Trained as an architect, he was influenced by medievalism, and founded Morris & Co. to revive the practice of handmade design and manufacture. After the Red House, Philip Webb designed several Arts and Crafts-inspired buildings from his London practice.

WINDOW **p.167** ROOF **p.168** CHIMNEY **p.169** STAIRCASE **p.176** GABLE **p.179** STONE **p.192** BRICK **p.195** GLASS **p.206** STAINED GLASS **p.207**

Neuschwanstein Castle

1869
–
1892

EDUARD RIEDEL • GEORG VON DOLLMANN: BAVARIA, GERMANY

Other key works

Hohenzollern Castle, Friedrich August Stüler, 1850–67, Baden-Württemberg, Germany

Schwerin Palace, Gottfried Semper, Friedrich August Stüler, Georg Adolph Demmler and Ernst Friedrich Zwirner, 1845–57, Mecklenburg-Vorpommern, Germany

Hohenschwangau Castle, Domenico Quaglio the Younger, 1833–7, Schwangau, Germany

High on a crag, on the site of two smaller castles, Neuschwanstein Castle was commissioned by King Ludwig II (1845–86), but by the time of his death at just 41, only one-third was completed.

After Ludwig died, the unfinished castle, with its pinnacles, turrets and roofs at different levels, was opened to the public as a museum. Simplified versions of the bower and square tower were finished six years later, and only about 15 of the rooms were ever finished. Built in brick faced with limestone, at a time when strongholds were no longer necessary, the castle represents Ludwig's passion for medieval mythology. Much of the design was based on aspects of two earlier castles, Wartburg in Germany and Pierrefonds in France.

Many features from medieval castles are used, such as tall towers, spires, battlements, machicolations and a walled courtyard, but nineteenth-century luxuries were also installed, such as running water, flushing toilets, a central-heating system and telephone lines. With its pillars of imitation porphyry and lapis lazuli, columns of inlaid stone and a vaulted ceiling, the two-storey throne room was inspired by Hagia Sophia in Constantinople (see page 62). In general, however, the castle follows the Romanesque Revival style that was particularly popular in Germany at the time. Evidence of that style can be seen in the round-topped arches and barrel vaults and its thick, strong walls.

EDUARD RIEDEL AND GEORG VON DOLLMANN
Eduard Riedel (1813–85) first studied architecture in Bayreuth, northern Bavaria, and graduated in Munich in 1834. Sought after by prestigious patrons, he became the leading court architect. Georg von Dollmann (1830–95) also studied architecture in Munich. In 1868, he began working for King Ludwig II, and in 1874 he took over the direction of Neuschwanstein Castle from Riedel.

ROOF **p.168**   TOWER **p.174**   COURTYARD **p.175**   COLUMN **p.177**   MOULDING **p.181**   SPIRE **p.184**
STONE **p.192**   BRICK **p.195**   GLASS **p.206**

Sagrada Família

ANTONI GAUDÍ: BARCELONA, SPAIN

1881
—

ANTONI GAUDÍ
A devout Catholic and skilful architect and craftsman, Gaudí was put in charge of the construction of the Basilica i Temple Expiatori de la Sagrada Família in Barcelona in 1884. Although he followed a mathematical structure for the building, he drew few plans, working mainly with models and his own impromptu and often eccentric ideas.

For Barcelona's Basilica of the Sagrada Família (Holy Family), Antoni Gaudí (1852–1926) created soaring pinnacles, expressive sculpture and dramatic façades.

In Catalonia, the Gothic Revival blended with Moorish architecture at the end of the nineteenth century, creating a style called Modernismo. Gaudí mixed these concepts with his own unique ideas and influences from the Spanish landscape and the arts of India, Persia, China, Egypt and Japan. Sagrada Família was the inspiration of a bookseller, José María Bocabella (1815–92), after seeing Saint Peter's in Rome.

In 1884, Gaudí was appointed architect director of the project, and planned the cathedral as a giant stone and glass celebration of the mysteries of the Catholic faith. However, when he died 43 years later, only 25 per cent of the cathedral was finished. Gaudí created many forms inspired by nature, but the entirety of the colossal building is intended to portray aspects of the Bible.

Although it forms a Latin cross, little else in the building complies with tradition. There are three monumental façades representing decisive events of Christ's life: the Nativity; the Passion and Crucifixion; and the Resurrection. Each has four tall towers, decorated with mosaics and glass, with bells inside them. The sculptures of holy figures are all modelled from ordinary citizens of Barcelona, while the towers represent the Evangelists and the Apostles. Multi-coloured mosaics and 'pompom' finishes on some pinnacles symbolize the mitre, ring and staff of Catholic bishops.

Other key works
Casa Batlló, Antoni Gaudí, 1904–06, Barcelona, Spain
Casa Milà, Antoni Gaudí, 1906–12, Barcelona, Spain
Park Güell, Antoni Gaudí, 1900–14, Barcelona, Spain

GOTHIC REVIVAL **p.32** ART NOUVEAU **p.36**

ROOF **p.168**   ARCH **p.173**   TOWER **p.174**   NAVE **p.182**   VAULT **p.183**   SPIRE **p.184**   PORTICO/PORCH **p.186**
STONE **p.192**   STAINED GLASS **p.207**

Wainwright Building

1891

LOUIS SULLIVAN • DANKMAR ADLER: ST. LOUIS, USA

Other key works

Auditorium Building, Adler & Sullivan, 1889, Chicago, USA

Reliance Building, Daniel Burnham, John Root and Charles Atwood, 1890–5, Chicago, USA

Carson, Pirie, Scott and Company Building, Louis Sullivan, 1899, Chicago, USA

Built to a design by Louis Sullivan (1856–1924) and Dankmar Adler (1844–1900), the Wainwright Building is one of the first skyscrapers in the world.

Named after a local financier, Ellis Wainwright (1850–1924), who needed office space to manage the St. Louis Brewers Association, the Wainwright Building is based on three parts of a classical column: the base, shaft and capital. It uses modern construction techniques, with an underlying steel structure covered by a terracotta façade. The ground floor had street-level shops with wide glazed openings; the higher floors had easily accessible offices; and the top floors contained water tanks and building machinery. All the windows are set behind columns and piers, emphasizing verticality. Decorative reliefs of foliage are carved in terracotta panels on each floor. The ninth floor features a frieze of winding leaf scrolls framing circular inset windows.

Sullivan wrote: '[The skyscraper] must be tall, every inch of it tall. The force and power of altitude must be in it and the glory and pride of exaltation must be in it. It must be every inch a proud and soaring thing, rising in sheer exultation that from bottom to top it is a unit without a single dissenting line.' Despite the classical-column arrangement, the building's design was deliberately modern, with the building's construction reflected through its simple geometric form and organic ornamentation.

LOUIS SULLIVAN AND DANKMAR ADLER
Considered by many as the 'father of skyscrapers' and 'father of modernism', Louis Sullivan was also a mentor to Frank Lloyd Wright. German-born American architect Dankmar Adler was an architect and civil engineer, best known for his partnership with Sullivan in their firm Adler & Sullivan, which became known for its innovative, functional modern buildings.

CHICAGO SCHOOL **p.34**

WINDOW **p.167** ROOF **p.168** TOWER **p.174** STAIRCASE **p.176** COLUMN **p.177** STONE **p.192**
GLASS **p.206**

Karlsplatz Underground Station

OTTO WAGNER: VIENNA, AUSTRIA

1899

During the second half of the nineteenth century, Vienna increased in size, status and population, and became a world capital of music, art, architecture and philosophy.

In 1894, the year in which he was appointed head of the school of architecture at the Academy of Fine Arts Vienna, Otto Wagner (1841–1918) was given the prestigious commission to design the new Stadtbahn railway network, which was to consist of a series of stations and bridges across Vienna to meet the needs of the thriving metropolis. Within seven years, Wagner had planned, designed and built the entire range of structures, and in 1899, his design for the entrance to the Karlsplatz station was constructed as part of this ambitious programme.

Partly above ground and partly below, it was formal and restrained, yet reflected the curving, organic Art Nouveau style of the time. Two pavilions face each other across the tracks. Under an arched metal-framed roof, stylized flower and geometric motifs form a decorative frieze. Marble slabs are mounted on a steel framework on exterior surfaces, and the building's colour scheme of soft green, gold and white was used by Wagner throughout the Stadtbahn. Focusing on symmetry and simplicity, the Karlsplatz was revolutionary for the time, and met Wagner's objective of creating a lasting impact in Vienna. It followed the artistic principles expounded by the Vienna Secession, which had been founded two years earlier, and of which Wagner was an influential member.

ART NOUVEAU **p.36** ←

Other key works

Secession Building, Joseph Maria Olbrich, 1897, Vienna, Austria

Hôtel Tassel, Victor Horta, 1893–4, Brussels, Belgium

Municipal House, Osvald Polívka and Antonín Balšánek, 1912, Prague, Czech Republic

OTTO WAGNER

From 1894 to 1913, Otto Wagner, a pioneering Viennese architect and member of the Vienna Secession, was head of the school of architecture at the Academy of Fine Arts Vienna. As an inspirational architect, he helped to make Vienna a city that embraced modernity, creating buildings with a combination of stylized ornamentation and constraint.

WINDOW **p.167** ROOF **p.168** ARCH **p.173** STAIRCASE **p.176** COLUMN **p.177**
MARBLE **p.200** GLASS **p.206** IRON **p.208**

Great Mosque of Djenné

1907

UNKNOWN, REBUILT BY ISMAILA TRAORÉ: DJENNÉ, MALI

An astounding example of the Sudano-Sahelian architectural style and one of the largest mud-built structures in the world, the Great Mosque of Djenné was originally built in the thirteenth century.

Constructed out of sun-baked mud-bricks plus sand and mortar, all coated with plaster, the building was added to some years after it was first built with two towers and an enclosing wall. In the 1907 reconstruction, three tall minarets were added to project from the *qibla* wall, which indicates the direction of prayer. Cone-shaped pinnacles top each minaret, and inside the prayer hall are 90 huge rectangular pillars and small, irregularly placed windows on the north and south walls.

The mosque stands on a platform that protects it from being damaged in the annual flooding of the Bani River below. Thick outer walls, in places about one metre (three feet) thick taper inwards, and eighteen rectangular-shaped buttresses, decorated with wooden stakes and topped by pinnacles, strengthen the exterior. Bundles of rodier-palm sticks are embedded in the walls as ornamentation and also for practical purposes, as they serve as scaffolding for the necessary repairs each year. The rodier-palm roof is covered with mud and supported by nine interior walls with tall pointed arches, while the plaster coating gives the mosque a smooth, sculpted appearance.

Other key works
Djinguereber Mosque, architect unknown, 1327, Timbuktu, Mali
Bobo Dioulasso Grand Mosque, architect unknown, c.1890, Bobo Dioulasso, Burkina Faso
Larabanga Mosque, architect unknown, 1421, Larabanga, Ghana

ISLAMIC **p.20**

ISMAILA TRAORÉ

Ismaila Traoré (dates unknown) was the Djenné's chief mason, and in 1907 was paid to rebuild the mosque by the French, who had taken control of the area in 1893. Although traditional in many ways, including its use of vernacular materials and palm-trunk inserts that project from the façade, the mosque's symmetrical planning also shows some French influence.

WINDOW **p.167** ROOF **p.168** ARCH **p.173** TOWER **p.174** STAIRCASE **p.176** BUTTRESS **p.178**
MUD-BRICK/ADOBE **p.193** PLASTER **p.203**

Rietveld Schröder House

1924
–
1925

GERRIT RIETVELD: UTRECHT, NETHERLANDS

GERRIT RIETVELD
As a child, Rietveld learned cabinet-making and from 1906 to 1911 he worked as a draughtsman for a jeweller in Utrecht, before setting up his own furniture-making business. His architectural work follows the principles of his furniture design, themselves drawn from those of De Stijl. In the 1950s he worked predominantly on social-housing projects.

In 1924, the Dutch socialite and pharmacist Truus Schröder-Schräder (1889–1985) commissioned Gerrit Rietveld (1888–1964) to build a house for her and her three children.

This small family home represented the ideals of the De Stijl group of artists and architects in the Netherlands in the 1920s. Making a radical break with all architecture before, the two-storey house features a ground floor arranged around a central staircase and a dynamic, changeable open living area upstairs. Schröder-Schräder had always been interested in the arts and knew what she wanted, but she had no experience or training as an architect or designer. Rietveld at first said that her request for a flexible living space would not be possible, but eventually he achieved it with a system of sliding and revolving panels that could be opened or closed to separate or expand rooms when desired, offering numerous possible variations.

The house is constructed of perpendicular lines and planes, with several balconies on its façades. The colours adhere to the ideas of De Stijl, restricted to white, grey, black and primary colours, with little distinction between interior and exterior space. Still following the movement's strict standards, even the windows can only open at 90 degree angles to the wall. The foundations and balconies are made of concrete, the walls are brick and plaster, while the window frames, doors and floors are made of wood.

DE STIJL **p.41**

Other key works
Café De Unie, J. J. P. Oud, 1925, Rotterdam, Netherlands
Interior of Aubette, Sophie Taeuber-Arp, Jean Arp and Theo van Doesburg,
1926–8, Strasbourg, France
Eames House, Charles and Ray Eames, 1949, Los Angeles, USA

 WINDOW **p.167** ROOF **p.168** BALCONY **p.170** STAIRCASE **p.176** BRICK **p.195** WOOD **p.196**
CONCRETE **p.201** PLASTER **p.203**

Bauhaus Building

WALTER GROPIUS: DESSAU, GERMANY

1925
–
1926

Founded in Germany in 1919 in Weimar by Walter Gropius (1883–1969), the Bauhaus was a school of design that aimed to bring industry, craft and art closer together, reforming how things are designed and made.

In 1925, Gropius designed a new campus for the Bauhaus when it relocated to the city of Dessau, adopting an asymmetrical plan with a series of wings or blocks. Each of these was shaped to suit its function, including workshops, studios, library, dining room, accommodation and lecture, teaching and assembly rooms. The workshop wing and vocational school were in two separate blocks of three storeys each, connected by a two-storey bridge containing offices, and a five-storey block containing 28 identical studio apartments as accommodation for students and junior masters. Sympathetically designed houses for senior masters and the director were built on a nearby plot (see page 43).

The building is mainly built of reinforced concrete with brick infill. Emphasizing function over form, there is no superfluous decoration. Its many large windows feature steel glazing bars, which were used to create the glass curtain walls on load-bearing frameworks that dominate the workshop's façades. A flat roof creates uniformity, while the colour scheme is restricted to grey, white, black and a touch of red on the doors. The clean lines of the design exemplify the industrial, minimalist aesthetic of the Bauhaus, and interior fittings were all made in the school's workshops.

WALTER GROPIUS

Berlin-born Gropius worked for Peter Behrens (1868–1940) before setting up his own architectural practice with Adolf Meyer (1881–1929) in 1910. He founded the Bauhaus in 1919, acting as its director from 1919 to 1928. Throughout his life, he continued to demonstrate the principle, first coined by Louis Sullivan, that form reflects function. In 1934 he moved to England, then emigrated to the USA in 1937.

MODERNIST **p.37** BAUHAUS **p.43**

Other key works
Fagus Factory, Walter Gropius and Adolf Meyer, 1911–25, Lower Saxony, Germany
ADGB Trade Union School, Hannes Meyer, 1928, Bernau bei Berlin, Germany
Dessau-Törten Housing Estate, Walter Gropius, 1926–8, Dessau, Germany

WINDOW **p.167** ROOF **p.168** STAIRCASE **p.176** BRICK **p.195** CONCRETE **p.201** GLASS **p.206**
STEEL **p.209**

Chrysler Building

1928
–
1930

WILLIAM VAN ALEN: NEW YORK CITY, USA

Other key works
Chicago Board of Trade Building,
Holabird and Root, 1929–30,
Chicago, USA
Empire State Building, Shreve,
Lamb and Harmon, 1929–31, New
York City, USA
Rockefeller Center, Raymond
Hood, 1930–9, New York City, USA

Designed by William Van Alen (1883–1954), the Chrysler Building was the tallest tower in the world when it was completed in 1930.

From the ground to the tip of its spire, the skyscraper is 319 metres (1,047 feet) in height and comprises 77 storeys and 3,862 windows. At the time it was built as the corporate headquarters for Chrysler Motors, it was the first manmade structure to top 305 metres (1,000 feet). Rising from a broad base, it becomes progressively narrower until it reaches the tapering spire at the top. Steel-framed, in-filled with masonry and areas of ornamental metal cladding, it is decorated with chevron, sunburst, fountain and arc motifs, black and white horizontal lines and geometric patterns. 'Nirosta' stainless steel – a shiny non-rusting alloy – features extensively in exterior decorations, window frames and the crown and needle, while the lobby on the ground floor is embellished with marble and chrome. All these aspects exemplify the Art Deco style that emerged from the Paris exhibition of 1925.

Van Alen had intended to top the tower with a glass dome, but found himself competing for the greatest height with the concurrent Bank of Manhattan building by H. Craig Severance. Instead he added the spire, which was prefabricated in four sections and hoisted into position in October 1929. With a modern vacuum-cleaning system and 32 high-speed lifts, it was also a world-leader in efficiency.

WILLIAM VAN ALEN
Van Alen took classes at the Pratt Institute and worked for several New York City architects before winning a scholarship in 1908 to study at the École des Beaux-Arts, Paris. Back in New York City, he became involved in a race with his previous business partner, H. Craig Severance (1879–1941), to build the world's tallest building.

MODERNIST **p.37** ART DECO **p.44**

WINDOW **p.167** STAIRCASE **p.176** SPIRE **p.184** BRICK **p.195** CONCRETE **p.201** GLASS **p.206** STEEL **p.209**

Villa Savoye

LE CORBUSIER • PIERRE JEANNERET: POISSY, FRANCE

Other key works

Villa Stein, Le Corbusier, 1926, Vaucresson, France

Tugendhat House, Ludwig Mies van der Rohe, 1930, Brno, Czech Republic

Pavillon Suisse, Le Corbusier, 1932, Paris, France

With its horizontal windows, pilotis, flat roof and open-plan interior, the Villa Savoye exemplifies the International Style.

Designed as a weekend holiday home, this is perhaps the most recognized work of architecture by Le Corbusier (1887–1965), and was created in collaboration with his cousin Pierre Jeanneret (1896–1967). A detached dwelling in the suburbs of Paris, the Villa Savoye follows Le Corbusier's principle that 'a house is a machine for living in'. It also includes the five points he defined in his 1923 book *Vers Une Architecture* (*Towards An Architecture*): a building should have pilotis, raising it above the ground; a free design that was not dictated by structure; an open floor plan; horizontal, strip or ribbon windows; and a roof garden.

Right: Le Corbusier's idea of building a house on plain white pilotis was in order to create space under the structure, conveying a sense of lightness while also creating a paved, covered area for the owner's car.

Below: Both stairs and a ramp lead up to the roof garden and sun terrace. For Le Corbusier, the screened roof garden was one of the most important 'rooms' in the house, where people could enjoy the benefits of the sun.

Right: As they indicate a break from the dependence on load-bearing exterior walls, ribbon windows – long, horizontal, steel-framed glazing – became emblematic of the new International Style.

Because of the Villa Savoye's mainly white exterior façades and long, horizontal windows, devoid of the usual structural constraints, light floods into its wide open spaces. While the building primarily features straight lines, the internal stairs curve in a contrasting fashion, and there are sloping ramps that create a sense of movement. The pilotis allow cars to be parked close to the door while conveying a floating effect and emphasizing the horizontality of the windows. However, problems have occurred with rainwater leaks through the roof because of a lack of downpipes or window sills, interrupting the streamlined aesthetic, and the white surfaces have proved susceptible to staining and erosion.

LE CORBUSIER
Swiss-born Charles-Edouard Jeanneret trained as an engraver before becoming an architect and changing his name to Le Corbusier, learning with Peter Behrens in Berlin and Auguste Perret (1874–1954) in Paris. A pioneer of modernist architecture and the International Style, in 1922 he established a practice with his cousin Pierre Jeanneret and became famous for designing elegant yet functional buildings.

WINDOW **p.167** STAIRCASE **p.176** PILOTI **p.188** CONCRETE **p.201** STUCCO **p.205** GLASS **p.206** STEEL **p.209**

Fallingwater

FRANK LLOYD WRIGHT: PENNSYLVANIA, USA

1936
–
1939

Dug deep into a rock ledge projecting over a waterfall in deep, wooded countryside, the cantilevered balconies of Fallingwater imply that the building defies gravity.

Fallingwater is one of the best known works by Frank Lloyd Wright (1867–1959), and was designed for a wealthy department store owner. Its dramatically jutting tray-like balconies and wide windows give generous views from the living room and bedrooms. Predominantly made of stone and concrete, it seems to be part of the landscape, and despite the heaviness of the balconies, which had to be strengthened with steel, they appear to float over the gushing mountain stream. Inside, flagstone floors and furniture – also designed by Wright – help to link interior and exterior. The result expresses what Wright described as 'organic architecture'.

Outside, stone stairs and a curving path link the main house to a guest house and car port, while inside the hearth is built around boulders found on site. Few of the windows have conventional frames – instead glass is fitted between horizontal red metal bars that run right into caulked (waterproofed) areas between the stone of the walls. Throughout, Wright created visual contrasts, such as smooth and rough textures, heavy and light materials, clear and opaque elements.

FRANK LLOYD WRIGHT

One of the greatest American architects, Frank Lloyd Wright first studied engineering and then worked for Louis Sullivan in Chicago. In 1897, he helped to found the Chicago Arts and Crafts Society. His reputation grew when he completed the first of what he called his 'Prairie Houses' in 1900–01 – low, spreading buildings containing rooms that run into each other.

MODERNIST **p.37** ORGANIC **p.38**

Other key works
Robie House, Frank Lloyd Wright, 1909–10, Chicago, USA
Solomon R. Guggenheim Museum, Frank Lloyd Wright, 1953–9, New York City, USA
Johnson Wax Administration Building, Frank Lloyd Wright, 1936–9, Racine, USA

WINDOW **p.167** BALCONY **p.170** CANTILEVER **p.189** STONE **p.192** CONCRETE **p.201** GLASS **p.206**
STEEL **p.209**

Seagram Building

1954
–
1958

LUDWIG MIES VAN DER ROHE: NEW YORK CITY, USA

Other key works

Lever House, Skidmore, Owings and Merrill, 1951–2, New York City, USA

Jespersen Office, Arne Jacobsen, 1953–5, Copenhagen, Denmark

Pirelli Tower, Gio Ponti, 1956–8, Milan, Italy

Set back 27 metres (90 feet) from Park Avenue in New York City, in a stepped plaza with two pools, the Seagram Building epitomizes the principles of modernism.

Designed by Ludwig Mies van der Rohe (1886–1969) the 38-storey steel and glass tower contrasts dramatically with the granite paving of the plaza. Above the lobby, the office spaces have flexible floor plans and are lit with luminous ceiling panels. These floors receive plenty of natural light through the vast panes of grey topaz glass that reach from floor to ceiling throughout the building.

The clean, sleek lines of the Seagram Building became a model for many future office buildings, exemplifying the International Style in a skyscraper. Mies wanted the steel frame to be visible, but American building codes required all structural steel be covered in a fireproof material, usually concrete. To hide this framework yet still suggest a structural façade, he created an additional shell of non-loadbearing metal beams to surround the large glass windows, using 1,360 tonnes of bronze to provide the building's distinctive colour. At the time it was built, the Seagram Building was the world's most expensive skyscraper because of its use of expensive materials including bronze, travertine and marble.

LUDWIG MIES VAN DER ROHE
After being apprenticed to Peter Behrens, Mies van der Rohe opened his own practice in Berlin. Avoiding ornament, his pioneering buildings made use of materials such as steel, glass, marble and travertine. From 1930 to 1933, he was director of the Bauhaus. In 1938, he emigrated to America where he established himself as one of the world's foremost modernist architects.

MODERNIST **p.37** INTERNATIONAL STYLE **p.42** BAUHAUS **p.43**

WINDOW **p.167** TOWER **p.174** STAIRCASE **p.176** COLUMN **p.177** MARBLE **p.200** GLASS **p.206**
STEEL **p.209**

Sydney Opera House

JØRN UTZON: SYDNEY, AUSTRALIA

1957
–
1973

In 1956, the government of New South Wales, Australia launched an international competition to design a 'national opera house' for Sydney's Bennelong Point.

A little-known Danish architect, Jørn Utzon (1918–2008) won the competition with a sculptural, curved building, featuring overlapping white roofs covering two large halls, that broke radically with the plain rectangular forms of modernist architecture. However, technical problems soon arose, largely in the creation of the curving sections of the roof that Utzon said had been inspired by the peeled segments of an orange. Eventually, in 1961, the British engineer Ove Arup (1895–1988) came up with a solution, proposing a concrete sphere cut into 98 identical rib pieces. Unfortunately, after various disputes with the Australian government, mainly over rising costs, Utzon resigned. He was replaced by a committee of three local architects who, among other things, changed the interior plan to make it more practical, but ultimately the bulk of Utzon's design went ahead.

The roof was created out of 2,194 thin, pre-cast concrete sections, held in place by steel cables and decorated with a layer of white ceramic tiles, some shiny and some matt. Giant glass curtain walls were made to join these roof sections to the floor. The building is supported by 580 concrete piers that have been sunk up to 25 metres (82 feet) below sea level. The interior is made of local pink granite and the vaulted concrete ribs of the roof create a fan motif on the ceiling.

MODERNIST **p.37** ORGANIC **p.38** EXPRESSIONIST **p.40**

Other key works
Yoyogi National Gymnasium,
Kenzo Tange, 1963–4, Tokyo,
Japan
Olympic Stadium, Günther
Behnisch and Frei Otto, 1968–72,
Munich, Germany
Utzon Centre, Jørn Utzon,
2005–08, Aalborg, Denmark

JØRN UTZON
Before establishing his own practice in his home town of Copenhagen,
Utzon worked for the Swedish architect Gunnar Asplund (1885–1940)
and for a year with the Finnish architect and designer Alvar Aalto
(1898–1976). He designed houses in Denmark before winning the
Sydney competition, and although he later worked in Europe, the
problems in Sydney made many wary of commissioning him.

Cathedral of Brasilia

OSCAR NIEMEYER: BRASILIA, BRAZIL

1958
–
1970

Brasilia, the new capital of Brazil, was built between 1956 and 1960, mainly by the architect Oscar Niemeyer (1907–2012) to a plan by his friend Lució Costa (1902–98).

Niemeyer designed the cathedral using concrete in sculptural organic-looking forms. With 16 identical curving columns that rise, meet and splay outwards to form a crown-like appearance, the exterior of the building is highly dramatic. Completely symmetrical, it breaks with all precedents. From outside, the white columns draw the eye up to where they converge, holding up a concrete disc that forms the roof, before diverging to form separate points. On top of the central disc is a cross.

The interior of the building consists of a single space of about 70 metres (246 feet) in diameter that can accommodate approximately 4,000 worshippers. Glass fills the spaces between the columns so that the interior is flooded with light during daylight hours. Although the glass is plain elsewhere, around the high altar are swirls and shapes of blue and green stained glass, designed by the Franco-Brazilian artist Marianne Peretti (b.1927). A plain white rectangular altar contrasts with the coloured glass and curving columns. The latter convey a sense of weightlessness from inside because each tapers at the top and bottom. A separate bell tower next to the building is made of a single concrete column, and narrows to a point at its tip where it supports a 20 metre (66 foot) horizontal beam that holds four bells.

MODERNIST **p.37** FUTURIST **p.39**

Other key works

Edifício Copan, Oscar Niemeyer, 1952–61, São Paulo, Brazil

Palácio da Alvorada, Oscar Niemeyer, 1957–8, Brasilia, Brazil

Niterói Contemporary Art Museum, Oscar Niemeyer, 1991–6, Rio de Janeiro, Brazil

OSCAR NIEMEYER

Born in Rio de Janeiro, Oscar Niemeyer was a key exponent of the Futurist architectural style, recognized mainly for his design of civic buildings in Brasilia. He also collaborated with other architects on the headquarters of the United Nations (1948–52) in New York. He was an expert in creating sculptural forms out of reinforced concrete.

ROOF **p.168** COLUMN **p.177** CONCRETE **p.201** GLASS **p.206**

Habitat 67

MOSHE SAFDIE: MONTREAL, CANADA

1966
–
1967

Designed by the Israeli-Canadian architect Moshe Safdie (b.1938) as a pavilion for the World Exposition of 1967 in Montreal, Habitat 67 was originally an experiment.

Exploring the possibilities of prefabricated modular units to reduce housing costs and create a new form of dwelling, the project had started out in 1961 as 'A Three-Dimensional Modular Building System' for Safdie's masters' thesis in architecture at McGill University in Montreal. Through his design, Safdie believed high-rise living could be like living in a village.

The complex reaches up to 12 storeys and consists of 158 apartments of 15 different designs that vary in shape and size. These are formed from one to four reinforced concrete 'boxes' in different configurations. In total, there are 354 of these prefabricated concrete units, created on an assembly line, stacked in various combinations by crane, and connected by internal steel cables.

Each apartment has one to four bedrooms and is between 60 and 160 square metres (197–525 square feet), with suspended terraces and skylights. Inhabitants reach them through a series of walkways and bridges, with three lifts for the top floors. Probably inspired by the vernacular architecture of Haifa, where Safdie grew up, each box is set back from its immediate neighbour, providing privacy, a roof garden and plenty of natural light. This makes the apartments both individual and communal, and an improvement on the traditional high-rise equivalent.

MOSHE SAFDIE

Habitat 67 launched Safdie into an international career designing highly innovative buildings. In 1954, his family moved from Israel to Montreal, Canada, and he attained his first degree in architecture in 1961. After an apprenticeship with Louis Kahn (1901–74) in Philadelphia, he returned to Montreal where he established his own firm in 1964, and then another in Jerusalem in 1970.

BRUTALIST **p.46** ←

Other key works
Hansaviertel, Alvar Aalto, 1955–7, Berlin, Germany
Barbican Estate, Chamberlin, Powell and Bon, 1963–75, London, UK
Walden 7, Ricardo Bofill, 1972–5, Barcelona, Spain

STAIRCASE **p.176** COLUMN **p.177** TERRACE **p.187** CONCRETE **p.201** GLASS **p.206** STEEL **p.209**

Montreal Biosphere

BUCKMINSTER FULLER: MONTREAL, CANADA

1966
–
1967

In 1965, the US Information Agency commissioned Buckminster Fuller (1895–1983) to design the American Pavilion, now known as the Montreal Biosphere, for the World Exposition of 1967 in Montreal.

Fuller designed a geodesic three-quarter sphere with a diameter of 76 metres (250 feet) and a height of 61 metres (200 feet), as high as a 20-storey building. For almost 20 years, he had been perfecting his designs for geodesic domes, fascinated by the material efficiency and structural modularity provided by what he believed would be a sustainable and easily replicated design format. The dome is formed by a two-layer structure of steel rods that creates an outer triangular system with inner hexagonal shapes. Each panel was sealed with tinted transparent acrylic panels and the internal climate was adjusted by computer-controlled shades to maintain a regular temperature. Fuller considered triangles to be the perfect form, and through his design he showed that it was possible to create a viable structure using only one-fiftieth of the materials normally used in a conventional building of a similar size. The tessellated triangles provide maximum efficiency with simplicity.

During the Exposition, the Biosphere contained six inner floors housing American exhibits, with four themed platforms on seven levels and a 37 metre (121 foot) long escalator, the longest in existence at the time. In 1976, a fire destroyed the dome's acrylic panels, and it now encloses a museum dedicated to environmental issues.

BUCKMINSTER FULLER
Buckminster Fuller was an inventor, designer, author and architect from Massachusetts. He published approximately 30 books, held 28 design patents and received 47 honorary degrees. He also developed numerous inventions, mainly architectural designs, and popularized the geodesic dome. In order to try to solve global problems, he did not restrict himself to just architecture, but preferred to call himself a 'design scientist'.

GEODESIC **p.45**

Other key works

Gold Dome, Buckminster Fuller, 1958, Oklahoma City, USA

Dome Home, Buckminster Fuller, 1960, Illinois, USA

Eden Project, Nicholas Grimshaw, 1998–2001, Cornwall, UK

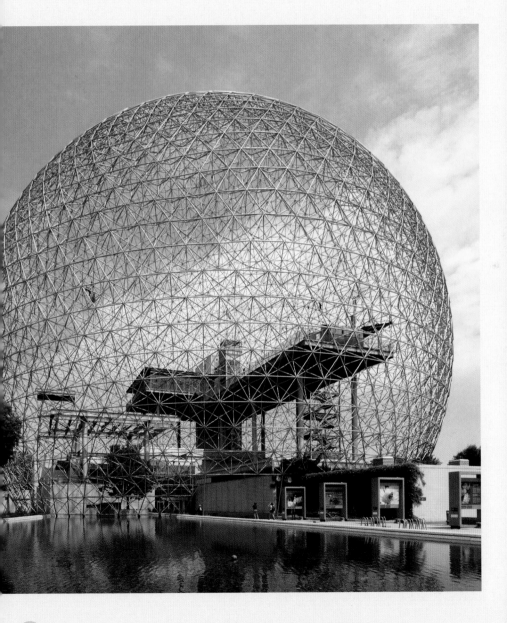

Pompidou Centre

RICHARD ROGERS • RENZO PIANO: PARIS, FRANCE

1971
–
1977

Influenced by ideas of the 1960s architectural group Archigram, the Centre Georges Pompidou in Paris is an exemplary work of High-tech architecture.

Housing one of the largest modern-art collections in the world and an extensive public library, the building was the winning entry in a competition for a multicultural complex, and was designed by British architect Richard Rogers (b.1933) and Italian architect Renzo Piano (b.1937), in collaboration with Irish structural engineer Peter Rice (1935–92). They created an 'inside out' building in an architectural style sometimes described as 'Bowellism'. From the exterior, the gallery resembles a giant machine, featuring an iron and steel exoskeleton of columns supporting a network of horizontal beams and diagonal struts, with large, coloured ducts. On the front façade, escalators are enclosed in clear acrylic tubes. The exposed services are bold and colourful, deliberately created to be noticed.

In comparison, the inside of the building is simple and spacious, with open-plan galleries and large windows, although a network of bright coloured tubes and ducts on the ceilings links the exterior with the interior. This High-tech approach was developed during the 1970s by Rogers, Piano, Norman Foster (b.1935) and several other architects who avoided modernist concrete, steel and glass 'boxes', and aimed to display modern technology and materials openly and honestly, rather than always concealing them.

ROGERS & PIANO

Richard Rogers studied at the Architectural Association, London and at Yale, New York, where he met Norman Foster. For a while, they worked together as Team 4 with Su Rogers (b.1939) and Wendy Foster (1937–89). Rogers went on to design several iconic buildings. The Genoan architect and engineer Renzo Piano has also produced several innovative designs, including the Shard in London (2009–12).

HIGH-TECH **p.49**

Other key works

Lloyd's Building, Richard Rogers, 1978–86, London, UK

HSBC Building, Foster & Partners, 1983–6, Hong Kong

875 North Michigan Avenue, Skidmore, Owings and Merrill, 1965–9, Chicago, USA

WINDOW **p.167** COLUMN **p.177** CONCRETE **p.201** GLASS **p.206** STEEL **p.209**

Portland Building

MICHAEL GRAVES: OREGON, USA

Other key works

AT&T Building, Philip Johnson and John Burgee, 1980–4, New York City, USA

The Humana Building, Michael Graves, 1982–5, Louisville, USA

Pacific Design Centre, Cesar Pelli, 1975, Los Angeles, USA

MICHAEL GRAVES

One of the first Postmodernists, Michael Graves ran his own architectural practices and was also a professor of architecture at Princeton University for nearly 40 years. A member of the radical Italian design group Memphis, he is recognized for his modern and postmodern buildings and for his product designs for Alessi, such as the 1985 Whistling Kettle.

Radical when it first opened, the Portland Building, or the Portland Municipal Services Building, is a 15-storey office building that abandoned the clean, stripped-down lines of Modernism.

The winning entry in an extensive competition, the Portland Building was designed by the American architect Michael Graves (1934–2015), and has a base, middle and top, following the classical orders. The exterior features a regular arrangement of small, square windows, and various surface textures and colours, contrasting with the rectangular steel and glass Modernist buildings that had dominated office architecture since the early twentieth century. The teal, terracotta and blue façade blends with the sky, earth and grass, while the boxy form of the building, with its columns, pediments and frieze-like decorative band, give it an imposing presence.

As well as breaking away from what was perceived as the boring look of other office designs, the Portland Building had to include offices for many of the city's public agencies, along with rentable office space and a food court, all on an extremely tight budget. Although the building is innovative, Graves aimed to echo architecture of the past, so the glazed terracotta element of the façade replicates a material common in historic buildings in Portland, and contrasts with the coloured reinforced concrete and fibreglass used elsewhere. This radical break with recent architectural trends was met with both praise and scorn, while its cut-price interiors proved problematic for occupants.

The Portland Building is closed until December 2020 for reconstruction.

POSTMODERN **p.47**

→ WINDOW **p.167** CONCRETE **p.201** GLASS **p.206** STEEL **p.209**

Vitra Fire Station

ZAHA HADID: WEIL-AM-RHEIN, GERMANY

1989
–
1993

The Vitra Fire Station is the first international work of
Iraqi-British architect Zaha Hadid (1950–2016), and it
displays her technique of mixing geometric shapes to
create a sense of dynamism.

The Vitra Campus is a vast complex of factories,
showrooms and a design museum. After a fire
destroyed much of the site in 1981, new buildings were
commissioned from major architects, and this time a
fire station was planned to reduce the risk of a similar
disaster. For the project, Hadid designed a series of
sharply angled planes that converge in the centre,
creating a structure that resembles a bird in flight.

The building was cast in concrete on site. Ultimately,
however, it never served as a fire station, as government
requirements for industrial firefighting were changed,
so instead it became an exhibition space. Overall, the
building is long and narrow without right angles, and
the walls appear plain and smooth on the outside, but
are punctured, tilted or folded on the inside. Hadid
emphasized purity and simplicity, with no added
decoration, embellishments, colours – even the windows
are frameless and there is no cladding or edging on the
roof. The oblique angles of the intersecting planes convey
a sense of movement, and the building appears to change
dramatically when seen from different perspectives as
walls seem to move and slide past each other.

ZAHA HADID
The first woman to receive the Pritzker Prize, Zaha Hadid won many
awards for her radical Deconstructivist designs, which often feature
interconnecting spaces and dynamic forms. After studying in Beirut
and London, she began her own practice in London in 1980. Her work
consistently pushed the boundaries of architecture and urban design
with new spatial concepts.

DECONSTRUCTIVIST **p.51**

Other key works
Heydar Aliyev Center, Zaha Hadid, 2007–12, Baku, Azerbaijan
MAXXI Museum, Zaha Hadid, 1998–2010, Rome, Italy
London Aquatics Centre, Zaha Hadid, 2008–11, London, UK

Moriyama House

RYUE NISHIZAWA: TOKYO, JAPAN

2002
–
2005

MINIMALIST **p.48**

Other key works
Funabashi Apartment Building, Ryue Nishizawa, 2002–04, Chiba, Japan
Love Planet Museum, Ryue Nishizawa, 2003, Okayama, Japan
Teshima Art Museum, Ryue Nishizawa, 2010, Kagawa, Japan

Constructed out of a group of white concrete boxes, Moriyama House deliberately challenges conventional schemes of domestic architecture.

Moriyama House is an experimental residential project located in a suburb of Tokyo, designed by the Japanese architect Ryue Nishizawa (b.1966). Formed out of ten white cubes or units stacked in an irregular pattern to create between one and three storeys, it is both a communal space, shared by six tenants and the owner, but also private, emphasizing relationships between public and private spaces. The four units used by the owner include a bedroom, living room, dining room, bathroom and an enclosed veranda.

As space is of a premium, the prefabricated boxes have extremely thin load-bearing walls, only six centimetres (two inches) thick, reinforced with steel plates to allow for large windows and to maximize interior space. Glass corridors mark transitions between different areas – no physical barriers mark boundaries around the building. Each box contains at least one huge window, but because of the ways the cubes are arranged, no window faces another, ensuring a sense of privacy. The spaces between and around the units are ambiguous. With its little lanes and courtyards, Moriyama House resembles a miniaturized section of city, and is one of a series of experimental residential projects designed by Nishizawa.

RYUE NISHIZAWA
Ryue Nishizawa established his own firm in Tokyo in 1997, having already co-founded SANAA (Sejima and Nishizawa and Associates) with Kazuyo Sejima (b.1956) two years earlier. In 2010 they won the Pritzker Prize. Working independently and with SANAA, Nishizawa has produced many innovative projects, developing solutions for urban living. He is also a professor of architecture at various universities.

WINDOW **p.167** ROOF **p.168** COURTYARD **p.175** CONCRETE **p.201** GLASS **p.206** STEEL **p.209**

Bosco Verticale

STEFANO BOERI ARCHITETTI: MILAN, ITALY

2009
–
2014

STEFANO BOERI ARCHITETTI
In 1999, Stefano Boeri, Gianandrea Barreca and Giovanni La Varra founded Stefano Boeri Architetti in Milan. Each of the architects has produced award-winning international designs, lectures on architecture and urban planning at major universities, and works with leading architectural magazines. They continue to design sustainable architecture across the world.

Two residential towers in the business district of Milan in Italy were the first example of a 'Vertical Forest', or Bosco Verticale.

The tallest of the two towers is 111 metres (364 feet) in height with 26 floors, and the shorter tower is 76 metres (249 feet) in height, with 18 floors. Growing on the terraces of both towers are 480 large and medium trees, 300 small trees, 11,000 perennial and covering plants, and 5,000 shrubs. The buildings were designed by Italian architects Stefano Boeri (b.1956), Gianandrea Barreca (b.1969) and Giovanni La Varra (b.1967) from Stefano Boeri Architetti, along with horticulturists and botanists, with the intention of reducing smog, absorbing carbon dioxide and producing oxygen in a built-up part of the city. It is an architectural concept that aims to increase biodiversity and promote an urban ecosystem, as the plants are inhabited by an estimated 1,600 birds and butterflies.

By improving the air quality of Milan in an efficient and cost-effective way, the towers are seen by many as being an important architectural step forward. The plants moderate temperatures in the building in the summer and winter by shading the interiors from the sun and blocking harsh winds. They also protect the interior spaces from noise pollution and dust from street-level traffic, and the buildings are self-sufficient as they use renewable energy from solar panels and filter waste water.

Other key works
Beddington Zero Energy Development (BedZED), Bill Dunster, 2000–02, London, UK
One Central Park, Foster & Partners, Ateliers Jean Nouvel and PTW Architects, 2012–13, Sydney, Australia
Via Verde, Fernando Ortiz Monasterio and Luis Gerardo Mendéz, 2016, Mexico City, Mexico

BALCONY **p.170** TOWER **p.174** TERRACE **p.187** BRICK **p.195** GLASS **p.206** RECYCLED MATERIALS **p.213**

Elbphilharmonie

HERZOG & DE MEURON: HAMBURG, GERMANY

2016
–
2017

Built on an old brick warehouse, the Elbphilharmonie is based loosely on an ancient Greek amphitheatre. Carved out of the ground, it mixes geology with architecture.

On the banks of the River Elbe, the Elbphilharmonie is supported by approximately 1,700 reinforced-concrete piles, retaining the façade of a defunct 1966 warehouse at its base. Above is a glass façade consisting of approximately 1,000 curved glass windows topped by a wavy roof. The combination resembles a hoisted sail, a wave or a giant crystal. It was designed by the architecture firm Herzog & de Meuron, and is a cultural and residential complex – at 108 metres (354 feet) in height it is the tallest inhabited building in Hamburg.

Overall, there are 26 floors, with the first eight inside the brick façade. A curved escalator from the main entrance at the east connects the ground floor with an observation terrace, the Plaza, at the top of the brick section, offering 360-degree views of Hamburg and the Elbe. In the glass storeys of the building are three concert venues: the Great Concert Hall, which can accommodate 2,100 visitors; the Recital Hall, which can hold 550 people; and the Kaistudio, which accommodates 170 visitors. The glass façade catches reflections from the sky, the river and the city, and contrasts in shape and appearance with the warehouse below.

HERZOG & DE MEURON

The careers of the founders and senior partners of Swiss architecture firm Herzog & de Meuron, Jacques Herzog (b.1950) and Pierre de Meuron (b.1950) closely parallel each other. Both attended the Swiss Federal Institute of Technology in Zurich, and between them they have produced groundbreaking and award-winning architectural designs, including the much-praised conversion of Bankside Power Station in London into a gallery of modern art, Tate Modern.

Other key works
Tate Modern, Herzog & de Meuron, 1997–2000, London, UK
Forum Building, Herzog & de Meuron, 2002–04, Barcelona, Spain
40 Bond Street, Herzog & de Meuron, 2006–07, New York City, USA

→ WINDOW **p.167** ROOF **p.168** CONCRETE **p.201** GLASS **p.206** STEEL **p.209**

ELEMENTS

WALL 164 • CEILING 165 • DOOR 166 • WINDOW 167 • ROOF 168 • CHIMNEY 169

BALCONY 170 • ARCADE 171 • DOME 172 • ARCH 173 • TOWER 174 • COURTYARD

175 • STAIRCASE 176 • COLUMN 177 • BUTTRESS 178 • GABLE 179 • ATRIUM 180

MOULDING 181 • NAVE 182 • VAULT 183 • SPIRE 184 • MINARET 185 • PORTICO/

PORCH 186 • TERRACE 187 • PILOTI 188 • CANTILEVER 189

Wall

KEY ARCHITECTS: JOHN NASH • GEORGES-EUGÈNE HAUSSMANN • CHARLES BARRY
EDWIN LUTYENS • ERNEST HÉBRARD • EERO SAARINEN • ELIEL SAARINEN

A structural element used to divide or enclose a room or building, walls can be load-bearing or non-load-bearing and can have numerous practical purposes.

Some of the different types of wall include supporting walls, cavity walls, curtain walls and partition walls. Cavity walls have two sections of masonry with a space between them for insulation and water resistance; curtain walls can be fortified walls around medieval castles, or external walls used to enclose buildings but which do not support the roof. Green walls have become more common since the late twentieth century and are planted with vegetation to help create new habitats and improve air quality.

The earliest walls were of wattle and daub, stone or brick, but Modernism saw the invention and common use of reinforced-concrete or steel and glass walls. While most brick and stone walls use some form of concrete or mortar to hold them together, dry stone walls are uniquely constructed, made just with carefully selected interlocking stones.

KEY DEVELOPMENTS
The main station in Finland's capital city, Helsinki Central Station was designed by Eliel Saarinen (1873–1950). Opened in 1919, it follows the Finnish Arts and Crafts style with imposing façades of thick brick clad in a pinkish-grey Finnish granite. Inside there is a mock-Romanesque portal on one wall, while other walls are punctuated with semi-circular windows.

Helsinki Central Station, Eliel Saarinen, 1914–19, Helsinki, Finland

ANCIENT GREEK **p.14** PRE-COLUMBIAN **p.13** GOTHIC **p.25** INTERNATIONAL STYLE **p.42** BAUHAUS **p.43**
ALHAMBRA **p.80** TEMPLE OF THE SUN **p.88** GREAT MOSQUE OF DJENNÉ **p.126**

Ceiling

KEY ARCHITECTS: DOMINIKUS ZIMMERMAN • INIGO JONES • JULES HARDOUIN-MANSART
ELIEL AND EERO SAARINEN • PAUL JOHANNES PELZ • SHIGERU BAN

*Széchenyi
Thermal Bath,
Győző Czigler,
1909–13,
Budapest,
Hungary*

Covering the underside of roof beams, or under the floor joists of the floor above, ceilings help to separate spaces, and prevent the passage of sound.

Ceilings can be made of many different materials, but wood and plaster are the most common. They may be plain or decorated with paintings, carvings or other ornamentation, and the joins between ceiling and wall may be decorated or concealed with moulded plaster or carved cornices. Many medieval cathedrals have vaulted ceilings, and some ceilings have exposed beams.

Coffered ceilings with patterns of recessed shapes became common in ancient Roman and Renaissance architecture. Renaissance coffered ceilings were created in a wide variety of shapes, with richly carved edges. During the Gothic period,

structural elements such as beams were often painted. During the Baroque and Rococo periods, fantastic and ornate painted reliefs, scrolls and garlands were also featured on ceilings.

Suspended ceilings, sometimes called dropped or false ceilings, can provide a useful space for services. However, some High-tech buildings deliberately expose the structural and mechanical components of a building on their ceilings.

KEY DEVELOPMENTS
The Széchenyi Thermal Bath in Budapest was built in a blend of Neo-Baroque and Neo-Renaissance styles following the designs of Győző Czigler (1850–1905). It is the largest medicinal bath in Europe, with water supplied by two thermal springs. The heavily embellished ceiling features metaphors and allegories about water, including stories about water gods and goddesses.

RENAISSANCE **p.26** ROCOCO **p.30** NEOCLASSICAL **p.31** POSTMODERN **p.47** ALHAMBRA **p.80**
PALACE OF VERSAILLES **p.102** POMPIDOU CENTRE **p.150**

Door

KEY ARCHITECTS: KUAI XIANG • JEAN DE CHELLES • PIERRE DE MONTREUIL
WILLIAM VAN ALEN • LORENZO GHIBERTI

KEY DEVELOPMENTS
As well as providing an entrance and exit, doors protect buildings and present a welcome or a warning. In Fez in Morocco, the massive royal palace of Dar al-Makhzen features brass doors that are ornamented with zellige tilework and carved cedar wood to ward off any external dangers and protect those inside. They are replicas of the 13th-century originals.

Blocking off or allowing access to enclosed spaces, doors have changed drastically over time, according to fashions, materials and construction methods.

The style of a building's doors can help to date the structure. Most ancient doors were made of timber, such as those of King Solomon's Temple, described in the Bible (I Kings vi. 31–5), which were of olive wood, carved and overlaid with gold. Unadorned stone or wooden doors in ancient Egyptian tombs were seen as the way to the afterlife, and many ancient Greek and Roman doors were also often plain, standing behind grand porticos.

Arched doorways became common in early Christian architecture, with pointed arches evolving in Islamic and Gothic buildings. Medieval castles were often protected with portcullises: large metal and wooden lattice-shaped gates that were dropped from above. Another lattice-type door is the Japanese *shoji*: translucent paper over a wooden frame. From the Renaissance period to the late nineteenth century, doors were often heavy and embellished with mouldings and opulent door furniture to convey grandeur. In general, simpler styles predominated throughout the twentieth century.

Dar al-Makhzen, architect unknown, 13th century, Fez, Morocco

ISLAMIC **p.20** GOTHIC **p.25** RENAISSANCE **p.26** BAROQUE **p.29** NEOCLASSICAL **p.31**
ART NOUVEAU **p.36** ART DECO **p.44** KRAK DES CHEVALIERS **p.76** PALACE OF VERSAILLES **p.102**

Window

KEY ARCHITECTS: EUGÈNE VIOLLET-LE-DUC • KARL FRIEDRICH SCHINKEL • PHILIP JOHNSON
KISHO KUROKAWA

KEY DEVELOPMENTS
Of the many window styles, two of the most common are sash, which slide vertically, and casement, which open sideways. During the Renaissance, large numbers of casements were produced in France, leading to them being labelled French windows. Large projects often combine a variety of windows. For instance, the Alhambra's Hall of the Two Sisters has a double-arched latticed window.

Alhambra, 1238–1358, architect unknown, Granada, Spain

Often arranged to be part of a building's decoration, windows are created to admit light and air.

In ancient China, Korea and Japan, paper was often used for windows, as glass window panes did not appear until the Roman era. Early Christian and Byzantine churches and Islamic mosques had glass panes surrounded by marble or cement, while Gothic builders introduced stained glass held in place with lead. In England in the fourteenth century, domestic buildings often had panes of flattened animal horn, but by the seventeenth century, glazing had become common in most buildings. This usually consisted of small panes, which were held in timber frames and often contained air bubbles, distortions and curved ripples, but in the course of the nineteenth century, these imperfections were largely eliminated.

In the late twentieth century, safety glass was developed, which made floor-to-ceiling glass possible. This featured extensively in Modernist office blocks, and double- and triple-glazed windows were also manufactured, with multiple layers of glass that acted as insulation. International Style architecture featured plain, steel-framed, horizontally emphasized windows, often in the form of ribbon windows that included right angles at the corners of buildings.

GOTHIC **p.25** RENAISSANCE **p.26** BAROQUE **p.29** INTERNATIONAL STYLE **p.42** DOME OF THE ROCK **p.68**
CHARTRES CATHEDRAL **p.78** TEMPLE OF THE SUN **p.88** RED HOUSE **p.116** WAINWRIGHT BUILDING **p.122**

Roof

KEY ARCHITECTS: FRANÇOIS MANSART • ANTONI GAUDÍ • CHARLOTTE PERRIAND
JØRN UTZON • FREI OTTO

Casa Battló,
Antoni Gaudí,
Barcelona,
Spain, 1904–06

As with various other architectural features, roofs can date a building. For instance, steeply pitched roofs were commonly built during the medieval period, the French Renaissance, the Arts and Crafts period and the Gothic Revival, while flat roofs were features of Modernism, De Stijl, the Bauhaus and the International Style.

Pitched roofs and pediments were typical of ancient Greek temples, while hammerbeam roofs were a characteristic of the Gothic period in Europe. During the Renaissance, multiple gables became fashionable in the Low Countries, while in Rome hipped roofs were more popular. The Mansard roof, designed by François Mansart (1598–1666) in France, was a four-sided hipped roof featuring two almost vertical slopes on each side.

In some Asian architecture, roof colours signify certain things, such as the black roof on the Pavilion of Literary Profundity (1776) in the Forbidden City in Beijing, which symbolically protected the valuable books inside if a fire broke out. Even if they appear to be flat, all roofs have a camber or incline to allow precipitation to drain off.

KEY DEVELOPMENTS
The main factors that influence roof shapes are the local climate and available materials, but some architects have been especially creative. For instance, the roof of Antoni Gaudí's Casa Batlló (1904–06) resembles a dragon's back, while that of Jørn Utzon's Sydney Opera House echoes the billowing sails of yachts in the harbour.

GOTHIC **p.25** RENAISSANCE **p.26** PALLADIAN **p.28** ART NOUVEAU **p.36** TEMPLE OF INSCRIPTIONS **p.64**
RINSHUNKAKU **p.100** KARLSPLATZ UNDERGROUND STATION **p.124** SYDNEY OPERA HOUSE **p.142**

Chimney

KEY ARCHITECTS: DOMENICO DA CORTONA • MATTHEW DIGBY WYATT • RUDOLF STEINER
ANTONI GAUDÍ

KEY DEVELOPMENTS
In general, chimneys became plainer at the end of the 19th and start of the 20th centuries, but Gaudí created some fantastical versions, such as the 28 chimneys on Casa Milà in Barcelona of 1906–12 (see page 36), which look like exotic sculptures but had practical purposes. Some were used for smoke, others were an early form of air conditioning.

Hampton Court Palace, architect unknown, 1515–1694, East Molesey, UK

The first chimneys appeared in large dwellings in northern Europe in the twelfth century, but they did not become common until about four hundred years later.

When the first domestic chimneys were built, fireplaces moved from the centres of rooms into the walls, and the smoke was conducted up the chimney through a flue. Chimney systems were built into the walls so that several fireplaces could vent through the same flues, often situated directly above each other on consecutive floors. Some of the earliest chimneys appeared on the roofs of large manor houses, usually projecting out from the exterior walls rather than being set back in them.

By the fifteenth and sixteenth centuries, it had become fashionable across Europe for the wealthy to include ornate chimneys

and stacks in their houses to publicize their wealth and prestige. These were heavily decorated, for instance the carved examples at Thornbury Castle, Bristol (1511–21) and the ornate red brick versions at Hampton Court Palace (1515–1694). After the Industrial Revolution in the late eighteenth century, tall, thin industrial chimneys became a common sight across many town- and cityscapes, used as a method of dispersing factory smoke high up into the atmosphere.

RENAISSANCE **p.26** BAROQUE **p.29** ROCOCO **p.30** ART NOUVEAU **p.36** RED HOUSE **p.116**

Balcony

KEY ARCHITECTS: AMBROGIO BUONVICINO • CARL KIHLBERG • ANTONI GAUDÍ
PAUL MANDELSTAMM

Enclosed by a balustrade or railings, balconies are platforms projecting from a building above the ground floor.

Most balconies are supported by corbels or brackets, although some are cantilevered. The earliest were made of stone or wood, then often brick, but in later periods, cast-iron, reinforced-concrete or reinforced-glass examples began to appear. In classical architecture, a recessed balcony with a roof is called a loggia, and internal balconies are often called galleries.

Galleries in churches or medieval great halls have traditionally been built for choirs or minstrels. In Islamic countries, the faithful are called to prayer from the top balcony of a minaret. In theatres, internal balconies and boxes are built with sloping floors to allow audiences to see the stage. Many public buildings have prominent balconies on their façades for important figures to make speeches or for ceremonial occasions, such as Saint Peter's in Rome (see page 90) or Buckingham Palace (1703–1855) in London. Some architects have designed sculptural balconies, such as those at Antoni Gaudí's Casa Batlló (1904–06) in Barcelona, which resemble skulls.

Casa di Giulietta, architect unknown, 13th century, Verona, Italy

KEY DEVELOPMENTS
A 13th-century house in Verona, Italy, is promoted as Juliet's home from Shakespeare's love story Romeo and Juliet. Its famous balcony was added in the late 1930s, assembled from parts in a local museum to cash in on tourist interest aroused by a Hollywood adaptation. However, the term Juliet balcony usually refers to a shallow balcony with no platform, just a railing or balustrade.

JAPANESE **p.18** RENAISSANCE **p.26** BAROQUE **p.29** ROCOCO **p.30** NEOCLASSICAL **p.31**
ART NOUVEAU **p.36** SUSTAINABLE **p.50** RIETVELD SCHRÖDER HOUSE **p.128** FALLINGWATER **p.138**

Arcade

KEY ARCHITECTS: GIOVANNI BON • BARTOLOMEO BON • GIAN LORENZO BERNINI
BENJAMIN HENRY LATROBE • THOMAS JEFFERSON

A series of arches supported by columns or piers, or a walkway that can be covered or uncovered, arcades were first built by the ancient Romans.

Aqueducts built by the Romans were among the earliest examples. Later, Romans constructed large arcaded walls such as those of the Colosseum, with its 80 arcaded openings on each of its three storeys. Arcades were also built in Byzantine and Islamic architecture, while in Gothic and Baroque churches, aisles were divided into a large arcade at the bottom with a further smaller arcade – the triforium – above.

The Romans also initiated arcades as covered walkways. Medieval cloisters were constructed of such arcades, and most Islamic mosques include arcaded court-yards. In Renaissance and Baroque towns such as Bologna, Padua, Venice and Turin, arcades line major streets and squares. The term was later adopted for enclosed shopping areas.

Blind arcades are superimposed against solid walls and were a feature of Romanesque architecture. Colonnades are similar to arcades: a row of columns joined at the top by an entablature, such as on ancient Greek temples or the colonnaded platforms at Angkor Wat.

KEY DEVELOPMENTS

Arcades or colonnades were a feature of many Venetian palaces, including the Ca d'Oro (1428–30) and the Doge's Palace, where the ground-floor colonnade is topped by a second running along the façade that creates an open loggia. Its curved and pointed arches have capitals decorated with dogs, lions, birds and acanthus leaves.

Doge's Palace, Filippo Calendario, Antonio Rizzo, Antonio da Ponte and Andrea Palladio, 1340–1580, Venice, Italy

ANCIENT GREEK **p.14** ANCIENT ROMAN **p.16** ISLAMIC **p.20** GOTHIC **p.25** BAROQUE **p.29** ROCOCO **p.30**
NEOCLASSICAL **p.31** DOME OF THE ROCK **p.68** CHARTRES CATHEDRAL **p.78**

Dome

KEY ARCHITECTS: FILIPPO BRUNELLESCHI • FRANCESCO BORROMINI • GUARINO GUARINI
THOMAS USTICK WALTER • BUCKMINSTER FULLER

Domes are hemispherical structures that evolved from arches, and first appeared in the ancient Middle East, India and the Mediterranean.

The earliest examples are found on huts and tombs, but the Romans were the first to erect large domes, such as on the Pantheon. Domes were important in early Christian and Byzantine architecture, and Byzantine architects invented pendentives to provide support when domes were built over square bases. They were widely used during the Renaissance and Baroque periods, when architects explored a range of different forms, such as oval and onion shapes. The latter are often higher than they are wide, and were used for churches in Russia, for

instance Saint Basil's Cathedral in Moscow (see page 94), but also appeared in Austria, the Czech Republic, Mughal India, the Middle East and Central Asia.

After losing popularity, domes returned to prominence in the Neoclassical period. From the late twentieth century, some architects began exploring unusual materials such as plastic sheeting or fibreglass, and new uses such as arenas, or the 'biomes' at the Eden Project (1998–2001) in Cornwall (see page 211). Buckminster Fuller's Geodesic domes (see page 45) are the only large domes that can be set directly on the ground as complete structures.

Santa Maria del Fiore, Filippo
Brunelleschi, 1294–1436, Florence, Italy

KEY DEVELOPMENTS
In 1418, a competition was held in Florence to design a dome for the cathedral that could span a diameter of 46 m (nearly 150 ft). Filippo Brunelleschi won with a proposal to build an octagonal dome without using a temporary support. He consequently constructed a self-supporting, hemispherical brick dome that remained in position inside the outer octagonal dome.

ANCIENT ROMAN **p.16** BYZANTINE **p.17** RENAISSANCE **p.26** NEOCLASSICAL **p.31** PANTHEON **p.60**
HAGIA SOPHIA **p.62** DOME OF THE ROCK **p.68** SANTA MARIA DEL FIORE **p.82** ST. PETER'S BASILICA **p.90**

Arch

KEY ARCHITECTS: EDWIN LUTYENS • CHARLES GIRAULT • JOHAN OTTO VON SPRECKELSEN
SANTOS DE CARVALHO • EERO SAARINEN

Used to span an opening and to support loads from above, round arches were used extensively by the Romans in viaducts, aqueducts, vaults and triumphal arches across the Empire.

An arch is held in place by the weight and force of each of the stones that make it. Some of the earliest examples date from the second millennium BCE in Mesopotamia. Curved arches comprise wedge-shaped stone blocks called voussoirs, precisely cut so that each one presses firmly against neighbouring blocks and holds them in place. The central voussoir is called the keystone. Pointed arches have no keystones.

The horseshoe arch, also known as the Moorish or keyhole arch, was first used in the seventh century by the Visigoths, and there are many examples of these arches in the Great Mosque (784–987 CE) at Cordoba (see page 22). This style of arch eventually also became popular across North Africa and later in Europe as an element of Gothic architecture. As well as the pointed arch, another common feature of the Gothic style was the ogee arch made of convex and concave curves, which create an exaggerated point.

KEY DEVELOPMENTS
Many arches are built as monuments, for instance the Arch of Constantine in Rome (315 CE). Paris's La Grande Arche de la Défense, initially called La Grande Arche de la Fraternité, is made of glass, concrete and marble, and was designed by Johan Otto Von Spreckelsen (1929–87) with engineer Erik Reitzel (1941–2012) as a monument to humanitarian ideals.

La Grande Arche de la Défense, Johan Otto von Spreckelsen, 1985–9, Paris, France

ANCIENT ROMAN **p.16** HINDU **p.19** ISLAMIC **p.20** MOORISH **p.22** ROMANESQUE **p.24** GOTHIC **p.25**
RENAISSANCE **p.26** MODERNIST **p.37** DOME OF THE ROCK **p.68**

Tower

KEY ARCHITECTS: GIOTTO DI BONDONE • GUSTAVE EIFFEL • ANTONI GAUDÍ
WILLIAM F. LAMB • SANTIAGO CALATRAVA

Leaning Tower of Pisa, Diotisalvi and
Andrea Pisano, 1173–1372, Pisa, Italy

From water to watch, from house to bell, and from Eiffel to Pisa, towers are buildings that have a greater height than width.

Often intended to convey impressions of power and to be seen from afar, towers have traditionally been built on castles and places of worship. They are space-saving, useful look-outs and are more easily defensible than lower, wider buildings, allowing great distances to be seen and attackers to be repelled. In the medieval and Renaissance periods, towers and spires on churches and mosques dominated urban skylines, and from the early twentieth century, skyscrapers did the same.

When it was built in 1889, the Eiffel Tower in Paris (see page 208), at just under 305 metres (1,000 feet), demonstrated that a metal frame could support an extremely tall structure. Forty-two years later in New York, the Empire State Building (see page 44) reached 443 metres (1,454 feet). Its mast was originally intended to be an airship docking station.

KEY DEVELOPMENTS
An important part of Christianity, bells to call worshippers or for celebratory occasions have usually been placed high in towers from where their sound carries. Some of these towers were connected to a church, and some were free-standing, such as the campanile of Pisa Cathedral, whose tilt began during construction caused by inadequate foundations on soft ground.

ISLAMIC **p.20** GOTHIC **p.25** RENAISSANCE **p.26** GOTHIC REVIVAL **p.32** ANGKOR WAT **p.74**
MARIA LAACH ABBEY **p.72** SANTA MARIA DEL FIORE **p.82** SHIBAM **p.92**

Courtyard

KEY ARCHITECTS: MICHELOZZO • ANDREA PALLADIO • ROBERT ADAM
FRANK LLOYD WRIGHT • TAKERU SHOJI

An enclosed space, open to the sky and surrounded by buildings or a wall has been a common element of architecture for thousands of years.

Courtyards have been built in many countries, for different purposes and in different shapes, including square, rectangular and rounded. Some of the earliest courtyards were built in c.3000 BCE in Iran, India and China. They continued to be built in both temperate and cool climates as they provide fresh air, light, privacy and often a sense of calm. Islamic and Moorish architecture in the Middle East and Spain often incorporated courtyards as tranquil and private spaces in the centres of palaces or other grand buildings.

Architectural features of these courtyards included central fountains or trees, with surrounding arches or arcades. In some Islamic cultures, such courtyards provided the only outdoor space where women could relax in private. Traditional Chinese courtyards are often created by individual houses arranged around a square. These courtyards are places of privacy and tranquillity, and almost always incorporate a garden and a water feature.

KEY DEVELOPMENTS
A spectacular example of Mudéjar architecture, the Alcázar is a royal palace, largely built for the Christian kings of Castile and León. Its Patio de las Doncellas, or Courtyard of the Maidens, is named after the legend that the Moors demanded 100 virgins every year from Christian kingdoms in Iberia. In the centre is a large rectangular reflecting pool, surrounded by sunken gardens.

Courtyard of the Maidens, Alcázar, unknown architect (bottom storey) and Luis de Vega (top storey), c.1364–1572, Seville, Spain

ISLAMIC **p.20** MOORISH **p.22** RENAISSANCE **p.26** MUGHAL **p.27** BAROQUE **p.29** NEOCLASSICAL **p.31**
KRAK DES CHEVALIERS **p.76** PALACE OF VERSAILLES **p.102** NEUSCHWANSTEIN CASTLE **p.118**

Staircase

KEY ARCHITECTS: DONATO BRAMANTE • MICHELANGELO BUONARROTI • ANTONIO DA SANGALLO THE YOUNGER • LUIGI VANVITELLI • GIUSEPPE MOMO • HERZOG & DE MEURON

Stairs appear in some of the oldest works of architecture, such as the Palace at Knossos, Crete, of c.1500 BCE, and these staircases can help to date a building.

The ancient Romans introduced spiral staircases and barrel-vaulted flights of stairs enclosed by walls. Many medieval castles contained spiral staircases built around a central newel or pillar within narrow towers. These turned in a clockwise direction to allow right-handed defenders a greater range of movement with their swords and restrict right-handed attackers.

In 1524, Michelangelo designed wide open interior staircases at the Florentine Laurentian Library (1525–71) that inspired many ensuing designs, and dramatic staircases became one of the defining features of grand Baroque architecture.

Traditionally staircases were built of wood, stone or marble, but the use of steel and reinforced concrete at the end of the nineteenth century made different structures possible. Unusual staircases include the one at Tower Bridge House, London, built in 2006 by Richard Rogers Partnership, and the winding staircase at Umschreibung in Munich, built in 2004 by artist Olafur Eliasson (b.1967).

KEY DEVELOPMENTS
Double-helix staircases consisting of two spirals evolved during the Renaissance. The Château de Chambord (1519–47) features a spectacular example often attributed to Leonardo da Vinci (1452–1519). Another sweeping helix staircase at the Belvedere Palace in Rome was designed by Donato Bramante in 1505, inspiring Antonio da Sangallo the Younger to design Saint Patrick's Well, Orvieto in 1527.

Bramante Staircase, Donato Bramante, 1505, Belvedere Palace, Rome, Italy

ROMANESQUE **p.24** RENAISSANCE **p.26** PALLADIAN **p.28** BAROQUE **p.29** ART NOUVEAU **p.36**
TEMPLE OF INSCRIPTIONS **p.64** PRAMBANAN **p.70** DOGE'S PALACE **p.86**

Column

KEY ARCHITECTS: VITRUVIUS • ANDREA PALLADIO • JOHN ADAMS
THOMAS JEFFERSON • JAMES HOBAN

Decorative, functional or both, columns are upright pillars consisting of a base, a cylindrical shaft and a capital at the top.

Columns are generally used in architecture to support structures such as roofs, lintels or beams, although the ancient Romans also began the practice of topping single columns with commemorative statues. Most columns are made of stone, usually multiple sections held together with mortar or pegged together through a central hole. Wood or metal supports are similar to columns, but are more often called posts or piers.

The base and capital of the column help to spread the load being supported. Most classical columns incorporate entasis, where they have a slight bulge in the middle, and they narrow towards the top, which makes them look taller and straighter. Ancient Greek and Roman columns followed the three orders of Doric, Ionic and Corinthian, although two more were added by the Romans: Tuscan and Composite. Tuscan are the plainest of all five varieties, while Composite columns feature both Ionic volutes and Corinthian acanthus leaves.

KEY DEVELOPMENTS
The official residence and workplace of the President of the United States, the White House was initially designed by James Hoban in 1792. In the 1820s, two porticos were added to the north and south façades in the Neoclassical style, designed by Hoban with Benjamin Henry Latrobe. With slender white Ionic columns on both sides, they convey both elegance and power.

White House, James Hoban, Thomas Jefferson and Benjamin Henry Latrobe, 1792–1829, Washington, DC, USA

ANCIENT GREEK **p.14** ANCIENT ROMAN **p.16** PALLADIAN **p.28** NEOCLASSICAL **p.31** PARTHENON **p.56**
PANTHEON **p.60** DOME OF THE ROCK **p.68** CAPITOL BUILDING **p.112**

Buttress

KEY ARCHITECTS: JEAN D'ORBAIS • WILLIAM JOY • GERHARD OF COLOGNE
MATTHÄUS BÖBLINGER

Buttresses are exterior supports to buildings, usually made of masonry, projecting from walls and reinforcing them.

Mesopotamian temples and ancient Roman and Byzantine buildings were usually strengthened with simple vertical pilaster or pier buttresses that thickened walls at particular weak points. However, buttresses became especially associated with the Gothic era thanks to the development of the flying buttress. These are curved piers that are connected by arches to walls in vulnerable places. They extend (or 'fly') to the ground beyond the wall, exerting powerful pressure, and so enabled immense churches to be built, with higher ceilings, thinner walls and larger windows. The heavy stone structure needed to hold up vaulted ceilings exerted tremendous outward pressure on the walls of such buildings, and flying buttresses counteracted that force. They start from the top of walls where groin vaults direct the weight of the roof, and carry that weight away from the building and down a stone column to the ground. Hanging buttresses are detached piers that connect to walls by corbels, and corner buttresses support intersecting walls.

Quimper Cathedral, architect unknown, 1239–1493, Brittany, France

KEY DEVELOPMENTS
Flying buttresses give many Gothic cathedrals in northern Europe their extravagant appearances. Those of Notre Dame in Paris (c.1163–1345) are heavy and dramatic; at Amiens (1220–70) and Quimper cathedrals they are more delicate. Their inventor is unknown, but once architects began to use flying buttresses they could enlarge windows, making buildings look lighter and more heavenly.

Gable

KEY ARCHITECTS: GEORGE GILBERT SCOTT • PHILIP WEBB • J. J. STEVENSON
C. F. A. VOYSEY

Gables are the exposed triangular section of a wall between the pitched sides of a roof on each end of a building.

On ancient Greek temples, they are called pediments. A front-gable describes a gable on the front façade, while side-gables are on the sides of buildings and cross-gabled buildings feature them on both the front and sides. Gabled dormers are gable-shaped windows set in roofs, while gables that extend above the roof line are called parapets.

In northern and western Europe, where steep pitched roofs are common, front-gables are often decorated with step-like or curved forms, for instance in such cities as Antwerp, Tübingen, Amsterdam and Tallinn. A similar type is the crow-stepped gable, also known as the corbie step, which is stacked in a step formation. Gables have been important features in the traditional architecture of eastern Asia, where they are often ornamented with projecting roof tiles, statuary and carving. Steep gables were common in the Tudor and Gothic periods in England and in nineteenth-century America, where the Carpenter Gothic style adapted elements of the Gothic Revival, in particular pointed arches and roofs, which created high gables.

KEY DEVELOPMENTS
Among the earliest and most elaborate examples of buildings with parapet gables are the late medieval town houses of Amsterdam. Often with curved sides, Dutch or Flemish gables first appeared during the Renaissance and continued into the Baroque period. The style also spread beyond Europe, to countries as far apart as Barbados and South Africa.

Gabled houses, architects unknown, c.17th–18th centuries, Amsterdam, The Netherlands

GOTHIC **p.25** RENAISSANCE **p.26** BAROQUE **p.29** GOTHIC REVIVAL **p.32** HANCOCK SHAKER VILLAGE **p.110**

Atrium

KEY ARCHITECTS: GEORGES CHEDANNE • FERDINAND CHANUT • CHARLES BARRY
SUMNER HUNT • GEORGE WYMAN • TOM WRIGHT

KEY DEVELOPMENTS
Today, the term atrium generally refers to a sky-lit central court rising though several storeys with galleries and rooms opening off at each level. Galeries Lafayette in Paris was renovated between 1907 and 1912 by Georges Chedanne (1861–1940) and Ferdinand Chanut (1872–1948), creating a vast Art Nouveau glass and steel domed atrium.

Galeries Lafayette, Georges Chedanne and Ferdinand Chanut, 1907–12, Paris, France

An atrium is a large space surrounded by walls or rooms, sometimes open to the sky but often covered with glass.

Early atria were common in ancient Roman buildings, particularly in large houses or villas, where they were centrally located, often with a *compluvium* – a central opening exposed to the elements – but with enclosed rooms all around. In the middle of the atrium was the *impluvium*, a shallow pool to collect rain water, situated directly under the *compluvium*. The Roman atrium was usually the most lavishly furnished part of the house and also contained the *lararium* (a small chapel), *arca* (the household safe) and sometimes a bust of the master of the house.

The west entrance to Saint Peter's in Rome is preceded by a large covered atrium, surrounded by colonnaded porticos, designed by Carlo Maderno. Glass-covered atria became increasingly popular in the late nineteenth and early twentieth centuries. Because the sky outside can be seen, changes in light and space convey a feeling of space and dynamism.

ANCIENT ROMAN **p.16** BYZANTINE **p.17** ROMANESQUE **p.24** RENAISSANCE **p.26**
NEOCLASSICAL **p.31** ART NOUVEAU **p.36** MARIA LAACH ABBEY **p.72** SAINT PETER'S BASILICA **p.90**

Moulding

KEY ARCHITECTS: GIAN LORENZO BERNINI • CHRISTOPHER WREN • BALDASSARE LONGHENA
DOMINIKUS ZIMMERMANN • JOHANN BAPTIST ZIMMERMANN

KEY DEVELOPMENTS

Many works of architecture are known for their ornate moulding, in particular palaces and churches of the Renaissance, Baroque and Rococo periods. Examples include the elaborate ceiling of the Rococo Wieskirche in Bavaria and the interior of Saint Paul's Cathedral in London. In both, archways, walls and ceilings all feature intricate moulding, often inlaid with gold.

Saint Peter and Saint Paul's Church,
Jan Zaor and Giovanni Battista Frediani,
1701, Vilnius, Lithuania

Continuous, usually three-dimensional bands that decorate buildings, mouldings have been used in many countries and many types of structures.

Traditionally, mouldings have been used to convey importance or elegance, to strengthen and protect joints, or to enhance, disguise or decorate another architectural element. They often embellish the edges of a projection or cover transitions between surfaces. Usually made from wood, plaster or cement, or in ancient Greece and Rome from marble or other stones, mouldings can be plain or carved in patterns, such as cable patterns, resembling twisted rope; bead-and-reel, which looks like a string of beads; or egg-and-dart,

resembling a row of eggs interspersed by darts. The ancient Egyptians used two types of moulding: the cavetto (a deep inward-curving form that crowned temples and decorative shrines) and the torus (a bulging semicircular form placed above architraves).

The Greeks were the first to exploit the decorative possibilities of mouldings, and from then on, most styles of architecture have incorporated moulding, although it is usually absent in the pared-down aesthetic of International Style, High-tech or Minimalist architecture.

ANCIENT GREEK **p.14** ANCIENT ROMAN **p.16** ROMANESQUE **p.24** GOTHIC **p.25** RENAISSANCE **p.26**
BAROQUE **p.29** ROCOCO **p.30** ART NOUVEAU **p.36** SAINT PAUL'S CATHEDRAL **p.106** WIESKIRCHE **p.108**

Nave

KEY ARCHITECTS: CARLO MADERNO • GIAN LORENZO BERNINI • FRANCESCO BORROMINI
CHRISTOPHER WREN • ANTONI GAUDÍ

Sagrada Família,
Antoni Gaudí, after
1881, Barcelona,
Spain

Adapted by early Christian builders from the form of the Roman basilica, the nave is the main body of a church, where the congregation sits.

Traditionally, churches and cathedrals were built from east to west, with the nave situated in the western part. The east end was usually where services were led, and was reserved for the clergy. The word nave derives from the Latin word *navis*, meaning ship, as during the medieval period it was thought that a nave resembled the upside-down base of a ship.

The ancient Roman buildings where naves first evolved were public spaces used for business and legal transactions, and they provided an ideal model for early Christian churches as these also needed large, central areas, in this case for pilgrims to meet and share news. The nave is usually flanked by aisles on either side, and there are often elaborately carved stone or wooden screens that separate members of the laity in the nave from the priests and monks worshipping and singing in the choir.

KEY DEVELOPMENTS
Drawing on influences from Gothic and Moorish styles, Antoni Gaudí designed the Sagrada Família to blend with his own ideas as well as influences from Spain, Asia and the Middle East. Forming a Latin cross, it has five naves. The central nave is 45 m (150 ft) in height, while the side naves are 30 m (100 ft) tall.

BYZANTINE **p.17** ROMANESQUE **p.24** GOTHIC **p.25** RENAISSANCE **p.26** BAROQUE **p.29** ROCOCO **p.30**
MARIA LAACH ABBEY **p.72** SANTA MARIA DEL FIORE **p.82** SAINT PAUL'S CATHEDRAL **p.106**

Vault

KEY ARCHITECTS: DOMINIKUS BÖHM • HUGUES LIBERGIER • PETER PARLER • HUGUET

First used by the ancient Egyptians, vaults are made from arches to form curved interior spaces.

Vaults became popular in ancient Roman, early Christian, Byzantine and Romanesque buildings. The Romans often created barrel vaults: single curved vaults that usually ran the length of a building. Groin vaults were developed using two intersecting barrel vaults. During the twelfth century, Gothic builders discovered that groin vaults could be made stronger with added skeletons or ribs fitted in the groins, which created pointed arches that could be made wider or narrower, allowing larger vaults to be constructed.

From the thirteenth century, ribbed vaults became increasingly complex as additional ribs were added. Symbolizing the vault of heaven, vaults were popular for churches and cathedrals. During the Renaissance and Baroque periods, architects experimented with creating vaulted ceilings using lath and plaster (narrow strips of wood and plaster) rather than traditional stone, which enabled grander vaults to be constructed, and produced smooth, almost sculpted curves. In the nineteenth century, iron ribs were increasingly used.

KEY DEVELOPMENTS
The two-storey octagonal chapter house of Wells Cathedral was built in two phases during the late 13th and early 14th centuries. It has a central column and radiating ribbed vault that is often likened to a palm tree. The central column is surrounded by shafts of marble that rise to a single capital of carved acorns and oak leaves.

Chapter House, Wells Cathedral, architect unknown, 1286–1306, Somerset, UK

BYZANTINE **p.17** ROMANESQUE **p.24** GOTHIC **p.25** RENAISSANCE **p.26** BAROQUE **p.29** ROCOCO **p.30** ART NOUVEAU **p.36** CHARTRES CATHEDRAL **p.78**

Spire

KEY ARCHITECTS: JEAN D'ORBAIS • HUGUES LIBERGIER • ROBERT DE COUCY
ANTONI GAUDÍ

Probably from the Old English word *spir*, meaning a sprout, shoot or stalk, a spire is a tapering structure on top of a tower.

Spires originated in the twelfth century on ecclesiastical buildings to point heavenwards and be seen from distances. To minimize weight and wind resistance, some were formed of delicate tracery. Chartres Cathedral has two at its west end, one in an Early Gothic style built around 1160, the other in a Flamboyant style in the sixteenth century. They were common in the Gothic and Renaissance periods, but then largely disappeared until the nineteenth century.

In 1822, John Nash built All Souls' Church in London as a circular classical temple with a spire supported by Corinthian columns, while in 1855, the nine-spired Dakshineswar Kali Temple was built in West Bengal (see page 19). As technology and building techniques advanced, more spires were possible. Gaudí designed 18 spires for his Sagrada Família in Barcelona, while the Central Tower at London's Palace of Westminster was designed to ventilate the building. From 1930, spires were added to skyscrapers, often just to increase height.

KEY DEVELOPMENTS
First built in the 12th century and then rebuilt extensively in the centuries that followed, Saint Olaf's Church in Tallinn was one of the tallest buildings in the world when the original Gothic-style spire was completed in the early 16th century. After several re-buildings, the spire now reaches 124 m (406 ft) high.

Saint Olaf's Cathedral, architect unknown, c.12th–16th centuries, Tallinn, Estonia

GOTHIC **p.25** GOTHIC REVIVAL **p.32** ART DECO **p.44** CHARTRES CATHEDRAL **p.78**
PALACE OF WESTMINSTER **p.114** SAGRADA FAMÍLIA **p.120** CHRYSLER BUILDING **p.132**

Minaret

KEY ARCHITECTS: MIMAR SINAN • EMRE AROLAT • MARINA TABASSUM

KEY DEVELOPMENTS
The Kota Kinabalu City Mosque is the second mosque in Sabah, Malaysia, and has an architectural design based on the Nabawi Mosque, the second holiest site in Islam, founded in 622 CE in Medina, Saudi Arabia. The dome is blue and gold, inspired by similar Arabic architecture.

Kota Kinabalu City Mosque, architect unknown, 1989–2000, Sabah, Malaysia

From the Arabic *manāra* (lighthouse), minarets are slender towers attached to or near mosques, from where the faithful are called to prayer five times each day.

Although styles of minarets vary by region and period, most are formed of a base, shaft and gallery, and rise in a series of circular, hexagonal or octagonal stages, each marked by a projecting balcony. Most have interior staircases, although occasionally they are exterior. At the top is a bulbous dome, an open pavilion or a metal-covered cone, from where the muezzin calls. The upper parts are usually decoratively carved. Another of their purposes was as a ventilation system for the mosque.

Visible from great distances, minarets can be square- or round-based. They vary from thick spiral ramps, as at Samarra (848–51 CE) in Iraq (see page 20), to structures that delicately point up to the sky, as at the Sultan Ahmed Mosque (1609–16), known as the Blue Mosque, in Istanbul, Turkey (see page 198). The earliest surviving minaret was built in about 836 CE for the Great Mosque in Kairouan, Tunisia.

BYZANTINE **p.17** ISLAMIC **p.20** MOORISH **p.22** HAGIA SOPHIA **p.62** GREAT MOSQUE OF DJENNÉ **p.126**

Portico/Porch

KEY ARCHITECTS: THE GAGINI FAMILY • ANDREA PALLADIO • ROBERT ADAM
JACQUES-GERMAIN SOUFFLOT • LANCELOT 'CAPABILITY' BROWN • THOMAS JEFFERSON

A covered walkway supported by regularly spaced columns in front of or around a building, a portico is usually topped by a triangular pediment, supported on an entablature.

The earliest porticos formed entrances to ancient Greek temples, and influenced many ensuing architectural styles. Ancient Greek and Roman temple porticos comprised a certain number of columns with set distances between them. These included octastyle (eight columns), hexastyle (six columns) and tetrastyle (four columns). For example, the Temple of Portunus in Rome (originally c.3rd–4th century BCE, rebuilt 120–80 BCE) has a tetrastyle portico of four Ionic columns. An even number of

columns meant an odd number of spaces, so the central two columns often framed the main door. A portico 'in antis' is contained between two protruding short walls (*antae*), with square projecting pilasters.

During the Gupta period of Indian architecture (c.319–550 CE), pillared porches were an important part of temples, usually lavished with ornament. Porches have continued to be significant aspects of public and private architecture throughout the world.

KEY DEVELOPMENTS
The English 'country house' is a large house or mansion set in the English countryside. Many were built in Palladian or Neoclassical styles and feature grand porticos. The Palladian Croome Court was designed mainly by Lancelot 'Capability' Brown (c.1715–83). The south façade features a projecting Ionic tetrastyle portico.

Croome Court, Lancelot 'Capability' Brown, 1751–60, Worcestershire, UK

ANCIENT GREEK **p.14** ANCIENT ROMAN **p.16** RENAISSANCE **p.26** PALLADIAN **p.28** NEOCLASSICAL **p.31**
PANTHEON **p.60** MARIA LAACH ABBEY **p.72** DOGE'S PALACE **p.86** VILLA LA ROTONDA **p.96**

Terrace

KEY ARCHITECTS: INIGO JONES • ROBERT ADAM • JOHN NASH
LUDWIG MIES VAN DER ROHE • PHILIP JOHNSON

Raised, external, open platforms, either near or attached to buildings, terraces have been built in many architectural styles since ancient times across the world.

Always open to the sky, the design and use of terraces vary widely geographically and historically, in style, construction methods, materials and dimensions. For instance, houses in ancient Egypt and Moorish Spain often had roof terraces, ancient Greek and Roman temples generally featured grand terraces in front of their porticos, and large terraces were attached to Assyrian and Persian palaces. One of the seven wonders of the ancient world, the Hanging Gardens in Babylon (c.7th century BCE) probably comprised stepped terraces. Traditional Buddhist, Hindu and Jain temples were terraced, as were Mayan palaces such as Palenque. The most important buildings of the Forbidden City in Beijing (1406–20), which was the Chinese imperial palace from 1420 to 1912, usually featured marble terraces, and during the Renaissance and beyond many large buildings included roof terraces or terraces attached to the rear with access to gardens via grand balustraded staircases.

KEY DEVELOPMENTS
Farnsworth House is a one-room weekend retreat in the International Style designed by Mies van der Rohe with clear floor-to-ceiling glass and horizontal slabs forming the floor and roof, all elevated above a flood plain on steel columns. A separate slab forms a terrace, connected to the house and ground by two sets of wide steps.

Farnsworth House, Ludwig Mies van der Rohe, 1951, Illinois, USA

ANCIENT EGYPTIAN **p.12** PRE-COLUMBIAN **p.13** BUDDHIST **p.15** HINDU **p.19** KHMER **p.23**
RENAISSANCE **p.26** INTERNATIONAL STYLE **p.42** BOSCO VERTICALE **p.158**

Piloti

KEY ARCHITECTS: LE CORBUSIER • PATRICK GWYNNE • ZEEV RECHTER
PAUL RUDOLPH

Columns or piers, usually made of iron, steel or reinforced concrete, pilotis support buildings above ground or water.

Used to elevate buildings, some of the earliest pilotis were instead made of wood, although these were more usually termed stilts or stumps. Examples of early buildings raised in this way are fishermen's huts in parts of Asia and Scandinavia, which are made of timber and constructed over water. Buildings on pilotis are also commonly built in hurricane- or flood-prone parts of the world. Sometimes they are used only under part of a building when surrounding landscape is uneven.

Generally arranged in a grid formation to raise a building evenly, pilotis can also leave space for driveways or parking. Aesthetically, they can lighten

the appearance of buildings or convey a sense of floating. In 1923, Le Corbusier wrote that buildings should function with the efficiency of machines and, in his 'Five Points of a New Architecture' in *Vers une Architecture* (*Towards an Architecture*), he expressed the need for pilotis. Pilotis form part of several of his designs, including his 1914 Dom-ino Houses and 1947–52 Unité d'Habitation in Marseilles.

KEY DEVELOPMENTS
Well-known examples of pilotis in modern architecture are the Homewood (1938–9) in Surrey, UK by Patrick Gwynne (1913–2003) and Le Corbusier and Pierre Jeanneret's Villa Savoye in Poissy outside Paris. As well as supporting the buildings, the delicate-looking pilotis lighten the appearance, contrast with the horizontality of the windows, and create an effect of floating.

Villa Savoye, Le Corbusier and Pierre Jeanneret, 1929–30, Paris, France

ANCIENT ROMAN **p.16** INTERNATIONAL STYLE **p.42** VILLA SAVOYE **p.134**

Cantilever

KEY ARCHITECTS: FRANK LLOYD WRIGHT • MART STAM • MARCEL BREUER
WOLF D. PRIX AND MICHAEL HOLZER • GIUSEPPE PETTAZZI

A cantilever is a rigid, protruding, generally horizontal structural element that is anchored at one end, usually to a vertical support.

Cantilevers are often used when columns would otherwise hold up the free end of the structure, and can be used in bridges as well as buildings. Creating a cantilever is usually more expensive than columns, but the drama created means that many modern architects consider them worth the extra cost. The roof of Frank Lloyd Wright's Robie House (1909–10) in Chicago is cantilevered, and his Fallingwater in Pennsylvania has large cantilevered balconies projecting over the waterfall below.

In 1937, in Asmara, Eritrea, Giuseppe Pettazzi (1907–2001) designed the Fiat

Tagliero Building. This Futurist-style petrol station resembled an aeroplane, with a central tower supporting two 15 metre (49¼ foot) cantilevered wings. POPS gas station (2007) in Oklahoma on Route 66, designed by the architecture firm Elliott + Associates, features a giant neon sign in the shape of a bottle, glass walls and a huge cantilevered truss extending 30.5 metres (100 feet) over the forecourt.

KEY DEVELOPMENTS

In 1997, WoZoCo, containing 100 one-bedroom dwellings for seniors, was built near Amsterdam by the architecture firm MVRDV. As Dutch housing restrictions forbid north-facing apartments, and with a height restriction of nine floors, perpendicular steel trusses allowed cantilevered apartments to be built on the north side of the building with an east-west exposure.

WoZoCo,
MVRDV, 1997,
Amsterdam,
The
Netherlands

MODERNIST **p.37** ORGANIC **p.38** BRUTALIST **p.46** POSTMODERN **p.47** HIGH-TECH **p.49**
FALLINGWATER **p.138**

MATERIALS

STONE 192 • MUD-BRICK/ADOBE 193 • BITUMEN 194 • BRICK 195 • WOOD 196

PAPER 197 • TILES 198 • BAMBOO 199 • MARBLE 200 • CONCRETE 201 • WATTLE AND

DAUB 202 • PLASTER 203 • MOSAIC 204 • STUCCO 205 • GLASS 206 • STAINED GLASS

207 • IRON 208 • STEEL 209 • ALUMINIUM 210 • PLASTIC 211 • CARBON FIBRE 212

RECYCLED MATERIALS 213 • COMPOSITE MATERIALS 214 • TITANIUM 215

Stone

KEY ARCHITECTS: PYTHEOS • MIRAK MIRZA GHIYAS • GIOVANNI BON • BARTOLOMEO BON
GIAN LORENZO BERNINI

Whether igneous, sedimentary or meta-morphic, stone is one of the most enduring of building materials, used extensively in architecture for thousands of years.

In c.2630 BCE, the step pyramid of Djoser in Saqqara was built of limestone. Khufu's monumental pyramid at Giza is also pre-dominantly limestone, with the Pharaoh's large chamber in the centre constructed out of red granite. Almost 2,000 years later, the Assyrian city of Dur-Sharrukin (c.720 BCE) was organized around stone courts and its palace guarded by winged bulls with human heads carved from tall stone blocks.

The Minoans and Mycenaeans built extensively with stone, and from 600 BCE most Greek temples were also built in stone. Doric temples were usually made of local limestone, while Ionic temples were more often made of stronger, finer marble. The earliest temples in India and Southeast Asia were also mainly stone-built. Kailasanatha Temple in Maharashtra, India, is one of the largest rock-cut Hindu temples, carved from a single rock from 756 to 773 CE.

KEY DEVELOPMENTS

Stone is the basis of many of the most iconic buildings in the world. For instance, the Colosseum in Rome is built predominantly with travertine limestone slabs; two stone shells make up the dome of Saint Peter's (see page 90); Borobudur in Java (9th century) is made of two million stone blocks; and Emperor Humayun's tomb in Delhi (1565–72) is primarily red sandstone.

The Great Pyramid, architect unknown, c.2589–2566 BCE, Giza, Egypt

ANCIENT EGYPTIAN **p.12** PRE-COLUMBIAN **p.13** GREAT PYRAMID **p.54** SANCHI STUPA **p.58**
PRAMBANAN **p.70** ANGKOR WAT **p.74** CHARTRES CATHEDRAL **p.78** ALHAMBRA **p.80**

Mud-brick/Adobe

KEY ARCHITECTS: ISAAC RAPP • JOHN GAW MEEM • ISMAILA TRAORÉ

Many ancient dwellings, mainly in Africa, Asia and the Americas, were built with mud-bricks, made of clay, water and fibrous materials such as straw, rice husks or grass and dried in the sun.

Bonded with mortar in the same way as conventional bricks, mud-bricks are one of the oldest building materials. They are also called adobe, from the ancient Egyptian word for mud-brick, *db*, and they have been used over thousands of years by indigenous societies in many parts of the world. Being readily available, easy to make, lightweight, economical and flexible, mud-bricks have often compared favourably with stone, which is heavier, less economical, more rigid and not always as accessible. However, mud-brick structures need constant maintenance and often have a limited lifespan.

They were common in Mesopotamia, used to build dwellings with mud extracted from the Tigris and Euphrates rivers, and from 3800 BCE in ancient Egypt, where houses were built with mud-bricks from the River Nile. Traditional pueblo architecture in the Andean region of South America, dating from c.750 CE onwards, is built from both stone and adobe.

KEY DEVELOPMENTS

An enormous adobe citadel in south-eastern Iran, Bam has probably been inhabited since the 6th century BCE, with further fortifications and walls constructed between 224 and 637 CE. In Mali, the Great Mosque of Djenné is distinguished by its dramatic architectural style, which includes palm branches within the mud-built walls and roofs to reduce cracking caused by drastic changes in humidity and temperature.

The Great Mosque of Djenné, Ismaila Traoré, 1907, Djenné, Mali

ISLAMIC **p.20** SHIBAM **p.92** GREAT MOSQUE OF DJENNÉ **p.126**

Bitumen

KEY ARCHITECTS: PHAEAX • VITRUVIUS • CHARLES GARNIER

Great Ziggurat of Ur, architect unknown, c.2100–540 BCE,
Dhi Qar Province, Iraq

Bitumen (also known as asphalt or tar) is a black, oily, viscous form of petroleum, a naturally occurring by-product of decomposed plants.

From the tenth millennium BCE, some of the first permanent structures were built in Mesopotamia, the region between the Tigris and Euphrates rivers in present-day Iraq. The first Mesopotamian culture to thrive was Sumerian, followed by Akkadian, Assyrian and Babylonian. They were the first cultures to build entire cities dominated by ziggurats, which were mainly constructed with clay, straw and bitumen bricks, along with bitumen mortar, as supplies of stone were limited.

Under Nebuchadnezzar II (604–561 BCE), Babylon was the largest city of its time, and its shrines, temples, markets and houses were mainly built with bitumen mortar. He also rebuilt the city's Etemenanki Ziggurat with seven tiers covered in bricks, then coated in bitumen, which reached a height of 91 metres (300 feet) – this structure may have been the inspiration for the legendary Tower of Babel. Although bitumen has not been used as mortar for centuries, it has been used to waterproof roofs and roads, when it is more usually called asphalt or tar.

KEY DEVELOPMENTS
The Great Ziggurat of Ur was probably built by King Ur-Nammu (r.2047–2030 BCE). It was restored by the last Neo-Babylonian king, Nabodinus (r.556–539 BCE), who rebuilt around the surviving base. The original core is of mud-bricks and bitumen mortar, now covered with later fired bricks and cement, but the original temple on the summit no longer survives.

WALL **p.164**

Brick

KEY ARCHITECTS: POSTNIK YAKOVLEV • BARMA • PHILIP WEBB • CHARLES BARRY
LOUIS KAHN • EDWIN LUTYENS

Monadnock
Building,
Burnham and
Root, 1891–3,
Chicago, USA

Produced in various materials and sizes, there are two basic categories of brick: fired and non-fired.

Fired bricks have been made since c.4000 BCE, initially in China. Sun-dried mud-bricks were produced earlier, bound together with natural materials such as straw. Once fired bricks became available, they provided a strengthening, protective outer layer on important mud-brick structures such as temples, palaces and city walls. The practice of firing bricks gradually spread – the ancient Romans constructed large brick buildings throughout their empire, and their legions even carried mobile kilns.

Despite the extensive use of bricks, it was not until the Industrial Revolution that they were mass-produced, in part for the building of huge new factories. In the late nineteenth and twentieth centuries, however, the increasing demand for taller buildings led to a greater use of alternative materials. Chicago's Monadnock Building (1891–3), designed by Burnham and Root, remains the tallest load-bearing brick building ever constructed. Brick provides effective load-bearing façades, and continues to be used extensively for small- to medium-sized buildings, especially in the industrialized world.

KEY DEVELOPMENTS

In order to create level courses, bricks have to be equal in size. Different countries have developed their own standards over time, and these can vary considerably. Engineering bricks are generally used in lower parts of buildings as they are heavier, denser and less porous than standard bricks, so they aid structure and strength.

ANCIENT ROMAN **p.16** CHICAGO SCHOOL **p.34** MARIA LAACH ABBEY **p.72** KRAK DES CHEVALIERS **p.76**
SANTA MARIA DELLA FIORE **p.82** SAINT BASIL'S CATHEDRAL **p.94** RED HOUSE **p.116**

Wood

KEY ARCHITECTS: EDWARD CULLINAN • KENGO KUMA • SHIGERU BAN • ALEX DE RIJKE

Extremely durable, timber can provide a strong structure and support its own weight, and its use in architecture dates back thousands of years.

Some of the earliest Chinese wooden structures were built with load-bearing timber frames, which were networks of interlocking wooden supports. From about 5000 BCE, mortise-and-tenon joinery was used to build wooden-framed houses in China, while farmers in Europe were constructing long narrow timber dwellings at the same time. By around 50 CE, the ancient Romans were building timber-framed structures in large quantities.

Also called post and beam, timber framing is a method of construction that employs a timber carcass as the main structural support. In Europe, the technique had become highly sophisticated by the medieval period, resulting in such structures as hammerbeam roofs, of which a prime example is in Westminster Hall, London (1097). In China, temples were usually built with a timber frame on stone foundations, such as Nanchan Temple (782 CE) in Shanxi Province, which is the oldest wooden building in the country, while Todai-ji Temple in Nara, Japan, is one of the world's largest timber buildings.

KEY DEVELOPMENTS
Now perceived as one of the most eco-friendly solutions, wood has undergone a resurgence as a building material. It is not toxic, it ages naturally, it is renewable, and relatively little energy is used in its conversion to building timber. Wood is also a good insulator, reducing the amount of energy needed for warmth inside.

Todai-ji Temple, architect unknown, 728 CE, Nara, Japan

JAPANESE **p.18** SHAKER **p.33** SAINT BASIL'S CATHEDRAL **p.94** RINSHUNKAKU **p.100** HANCOCK SHAKER VILLAGE **p.110**

Paper

KEY ARCHITECTS: ALEXANDER BRODSKY • SHIGERU BAN

Often used in the traditional architecture of Japan, China and parts of Asia, paper conveys a sense of lightness.

Ancient Chinese, Korean and Japanese architecture frequently included paper windows. The 'aesthetic ideal of emptiness' arose from Taoism, which began in China sometime during the fourth and third centuries BCE and spread to Japan, Korea and Vietnam. Traditional Japanese interiors often feature translucent paper walls called *fusuma* and *shoji* screens that run on wooden rails and can close or open spaces.

In 1995, after the Kobe earthquake, Shigeru Ban (b.1957) designed Paper Log Houses, each comprising 110 paper tubes. In 1998, he built 50 emergency paper shelters in Rwanda after the civil war, and the following year, his paper houses were built for the Turkish people after another catastrophic earthquake. In 2001, they were also built in India after the Gujarat earthquake. Inexpensive and easy to construct, Ban's houses have saved many lives. In 1995, he also designed a church for Kobe made of 58 cardboard tubes. In using recycled materials, Ban's paper buildings help to protect the environment.

KEY DEVELOPMENTS

The form of the traditional Korean house, or *hanok*, varies in different regions, but all feature *hanji*, a mulberry-bark paper that can be used on every flat interior surface. It has an excellent insulating capacity, is translucent, has air holes for ventilation, adjusts humidity levels and also acts as an air purifier by trapping floating dust particles.

Hanok, architect unknown, 13th century, Seoul, South Korea

JAPANESE **p.18** RINSHUNKAKU **p.100**

Tiles

KEY ARCHITECTS: SEDEFKAR MEHMED AGHA • MIMAR SINAN • LUIS BARRAGÁN
DANIEL LIBESKIND

Sultan Ahmed (Blue) Mosque, Sedefkar Mehmed Agha, 1609–16, Istanbul, Turkey

Usually used for covering roofs, floors or walls, tiles are flat manufactured slabs of ceramic, stone, metal or glass, produced in diverse shapes.

Traditionally made from local materials such as terracotta or slate, roof tiles appeared later than interior tiles, which were already in use on buildings in Mesopotamia and ancient Egypt. For instance, blue faïence tiles lined the underground corridors of the step pyramid of Djoser in Saqqara (c.2630 BCE), while the roof tiles of the Forbidden City in Beijing (1406–20) had symbolic coloured glazes. For instance, yellow roof tiles represented the Emperor, and green symbolized the Crown Prince.

During the thirteenth century, lead-glazed tiles were laid on floors of ecclesiastical buildings throughout northern Europe.

Tin-glazed tiles, known as majolica in Italy and delftware in Holland and England, were originally created by Islamic potters in the Middle East. In the sixteenth and seventeenth centuries, the Turkish town of Iznik began producing colourful tiles that were used in palaces and mosques. Until the middle of the eighteenth century, tiles were made and decorated by hand, but after the Industrial Revolution, most were machine-made.

KEY DEVELOPMENTS

The interior of the Blue Mosque in Istanbul is lined with over 20,000 ceramic tiles made at Iznik in Turkey. Iznik tiles have a fritware body painted with cobalt blue under a transparent lead glaze. The designs combine traditional Ottoman arabesque shapes with Chinese patterns, and their blue colour gave the mosque its nickname.

ANCIENT EGYPTIAN **p.12** BYZANTINE **p.17** HAGIA SOPHIA **p.62** DOME OF THE ROCK **p.68** ALHAMBRA **p.80** SYDNEY OPERA HOUSE **p.142** PORTLAND BUILDING **p.152**

Bamboo

KEY ARCHITECTS: KENGO KUMA • MARCO CASAGRANDE • VO TRONG NGHIA
ANNA HERINGER

Bamboo has traditionally been used as a construction material, for instance in parts of Asia, Oceania and Central and South America.

Because it thrives in water, bamboo can withstand extremely wet environments. Its strength, flexibility and abundance have made it a good alternative to concrete and steel, especially in flood- and earthquake-prone areas. In China, it has often been used as scaffolding and for simple suspension bridges – one example in the Qian-Xian area dates back at least to 960 CE and may be much older. Raised on stilts, traditional bamboo nipa huts (*bahay-kubo*) in the Philippines had a long history well before the arrival of Spaniards in 1571, and similar housing has been built in parts of Indonesia and Malaysia.

Although the use of bamboo in architecture diminished during the twentieth century, it has become popular once again today as environmental considerations grow and natural materials are increasingly favoured. The world's largest bamboo dome was built as the Indian Pavilion at Expo 2010 in Shanghai to demonstrate the synergy between urban and rural regions.

Batak House, architect unknown, c.1900, Sumatra, Indonesia

KEY DEVELOPMENTS

Batak architecture in Sumatra uses bamboo extensively. Batak buildings comprise the *bale* (meeting hall), *rumah* (house) and *sopo* (rice barn). The *rumah* houses several families in a shared living space. Toba Batak houses around Lake Toba have carved gables and dramatically curving roof ridges, while Karo Batak houses further north are built in tiers.

← JAPANESE **p.18**

Marble

KEY ARCHITECTS: PHIDIAS • JACOB VAN CAMPEN • THOMAS LINCOLN CASEY
HENRY BACON • FARIBORZ SAHBA

Because it is able to bear great weight, marble has been used in architecture for thousands of years.

Although the word marble derives from a Greek word meaning 'a snow white and spotless stone', it forms in various colours depending on impurities in the limestone. The first building constructed entirely of marble was the Athenian Treasury, built at some time between 510 and 490 BCE. The Parthenon was also created in pure white marble, quarried from nearby Mount Pentelicus. White marbles were reserved for public buildings and temples in the classical period in Greece (approximately fifth century BCE). Later, from the fourth to third centuries BCE (the late classical and Hellenistic periods), coloured marble was also used, but was mainly confined to interiors.

Roman use of marble spread from important public buildings to the homes of the upper classes, but remained a symbol of luxury, an association that continues today. For instance, in the US, the Washington Monument, built between 1848 and 1884, and the Lincoln Memorial, built between 1914 and 1922, are both constructed in a range of marbles.

KEY DEVELOPMENTS
Translucent white marble from Makrana, Rajasthan was used extensively throughout the Taj Mahal – this marble was also used for the Victoria Memorial in Kolkata, built from 1906 to 1921. Overall, 28 types of precious and semi-precious stones were inlaid into the white surfaces of the Taj Mahal, including jade, jasper, crystal, turquoise, carnelian, sapphire and lapis lazuli.

Taj Mahal, possibly Ustad Ahmad Lahori, 1632–48, Agra, India

ANCIENT GREEK **p.14** ANCIENT ROMAN **p.16** PARTHENON **p.56** TEMPLE OF INSCRIPTIONS **p.64**
SANTA MARIA DEL FIORE **p.82** TAJ MAHAL **p.98** PALACE OF VERSAILLES **p.102**

Concrete

KEY ARCHITECTS: LE CORBUSIER • LOUIS KAHN • TADAO ANDO • ZAHA HADID
SANTIAGO CALATRAVA

A paste that gradually hardens, concrete is strong and pliable, and the most commonly used building material of human origin in the world.

When cement, sand, stones and water are combined, a chemical reaction occurs, making the result – concrete – stronger than any one of its components. The Bedouins in southern Syria and northern Jordan pioneered a form of concrete as early as c.6500 BCE. Centuries later, the ancient Egyptians made a similar composite of lime and gypsum, and later still the Romans made their own concrete with quicklime, pozzolana and an aggregate of pumice, gravel, sand or rock, which they called *opus caementicium*. After the decline of the Roman Empire, however, the use of concrete diminished. In the mid-nineteenth century, two Frenchmen, François Coignet (1814–88) and Joseph Monier (1823–1926) were the first to use iron-reinforced concrete. Steel-reinforced concrete followed, with reinforcing steel rods, bars or mesh laid inside the concrete to strengthen it and absorb stresses caused by forces such as wind or earthquakes. Reinforced concrete revolutionized the construction industry, enabling huge skyscrapers and sculpted works of architecture to be created.

KEY DEVELOPMENTS
To commemorate the 100th anniversary of Himeji becoming a municipality, Tadao Ando designed the Museum of Literature. Using reinforced concrete, stone and glass on the exterior and wood inside, he created the building as two cubes and a cylinder. Three years after completion, he designed an additional annex as another concrete box and a glass cube.

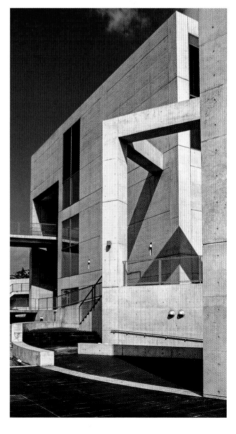

Himeji City Museum of Literature, Tadao Ando, 1989–96, Hyogo Prefecture, Japan

ANCIENT ROMAN **p.16** PANTHEON **p.60** SAINT PETER'S BASILICA **p.90** FALLINGWATER **p.138** SYDNEY OPERA HOUSE **p.142** HABITAT 67 **p.146**

Wattle and Daub

KEY ARCHITECTS: NONE KNOWN

Shakespeare's Birthplace, architect unknown, 16th century, Stratford-upon-Avon, UK

From approximately 6,000 years ago until about 400 years ago, in parts of Europe, Asia, America, Australia and Africa, many dwellings were made of wattle and daub.

Wattle and daub is a method of constructing walls with a woven lattice of wooden strips called wattle, which is then daubed with a sticky mixture that may include such ingredients as mud, clay, sand, animal dung and straw. As it dries, this composite hardens into a waterproof covering.

Sometimes wattle and daub is used as a filler for timber-framed structures, as at Shakespeare's Birthplace in Stratford-upon-Avon in the UK. In such timber-framed wattle and daub buildings, a series of vertical wooden staves or stakes are driven into the ground and crossed with horizontal beams or lintels. Sometimes the wattle was made by weaving thin branches between the upright stakes, and sometimes it was slotted in the framework as loose panels. The daub was applied simultaneously from both sides in damp balls, and pressed into and around the wattle. As it hardened, it was usually covered with a coating of plaster.

KEY DEVELOPMENTS

Local materials are always used, so willow, reeds or bamboo have all been employed for the wattle depending on availability. Although made up of different components, daub always includes binders such as clay; aggregates for bulk and stability, such as earth or sand; and reinforcement to hold it all together, such as straw or dung.

SHIBAM **p.92**

Plaster

KEY ARCHITECTS: PIERRE CHAMBIGES • ROBERT ADAM • HONORÉ DAUMET
CHALERMCHAI KOSITPIPAT

Wat Rong Khun,
Chalermchai
Kositpipat, 1996,
Chiang Rai,
Thailand

Used in architectural construction for centuries, plaster is a mixture of lime or gypsum, plus water and sand, which hardens on drying.

The ancient Egyptians used a plaster made from calcined gypsum; the Mycenaeans used a fine lime plaster; and by the fifth century BCE, lime plaster was frequently used on Greek temples. The ancient Romans used mixtures of lime and sand for initial layers, over which they applied a finer mixture of gypsum, lime, sand and marble dust, but after the fall of the Roman Empire, the addition of marble dust was abandoned until the Renaissance.

During the medieval period in Europe, both lime and gypsum plaster were used extensively to decorate or to smooth and protect important buildings, often with such things as hair added as a strengthening agent. Until the early twentieth century, lime was the predominant binder as it was cheaper and more accessible than gypsum, but the latter became more widely available after World War I. Because of extensive mining of gypsum around Paris, it became known as plaster of Paris.

KEY DEVELOPMENTS

Wat Rong Khun, known as the White Temple, in Chiang Rai is made of white plaster with small pieces of broken glass embedded in its surface so that it glitters in the sun. White signifies the Buddha's purity and the glass symbolizes the Buddha's wisdom and teachings. The intricately shaped temple was designed and constructed by Thai artist Chalermchai Kositpipat (b.1955).

ANCIENT EGYPTIAN **p.12** ANCIENT ROMAN **p.16** RENAISSANCE **p.26**

Mosaic

KEY ARCHITECTS: ANTONI GAUDÍ • SQUIRE J. VICKERS • JOSEP MARIA JUJOL I GIBERT
SIMON RODIA

Most mosaics are made of small, square pieces of coloured stone or glass called tesserae, although 'pebble mosaics' are made of small rounded pieces of stone on floors.

The earliest known mosaics date from the second half of the third millennium BCE, made of stones, shells and ivory for a temple in Tell Al-'Ubaid, Mesopotamia. Mosaics became widespread in ancient Greece and Rome, and the Romans developed a particular technique of making pictures on floors and walls out of coloured glass tesserae, often backed with gold foil.

From the fourth century onwards, Christian and Byzantine basilicas were frequently decorated with mosaics. Fifth- and sixth-century synagogues in the Middle East were decorated with Byzantine- and Roman-influenced floor mosaics, while patterned mosaics were also widely used in early Islamic religious buildings and palaces, including the Dome of the Rock in Jerusalem and the Umayyad Mosque (715 CE) in Damascus. Trencadís is another type of mosaic, made from pieces of broken tile, chinaware and glass. Antoni Gaudí used it to great effect, for instance at Park Güell (1900–14) in Barcelona.

Church of San Vitale, architect unknown, 527–47 CE, Ravenna, Italy

KEY DEVELOPMENTS
The Basilica of San Vitale in Ravenna is an important example of early Christian Byzantine art and architecture. The richly coloured, intricate mosaics were executed soon after the Byzantine conquest of the city, and depict Emperor Justinian I and Empress Theodora, Jesus and his apostles, and Saints Gervasius and Protasius, among others, along with decorative medallions of flowers and fruit.

ANCIENT GREEK **p.14** ANCIENT ROMAN **p.16** BYZANTINE **p.17** ART NOUVEAU **p.36**
DOME OF THE ROCK **p.68** SAGRADA FAMÍLIA **p.120**

Stucco

KEY ARCHITECTS: DOMINIKUS ZIMMERMANN • JOHANN BAPTIST ZIMMERMANN
ANDREA PALLADIO • ROBERT ADAM • ADOLF LOOS • LE CORBUSIER

Although in the Italian language stucco can mean both plaster and stucco, there are significant differences in the composition and usage of the two materials.

Traditional stucco, like plaster, was made of lime, sand and water, but in 1824, English manufacturer Joseph Aspdin (1778–1855) invented and patented what he called Portland cement, which produced harder stucco and soon came to replace the lime in the mix. Similarly, plaster increasingly included gypsum rather than lime.

Stucco is more often used on the exterior of buildings, with plaster on interiors. Sometimes additives such as acrylics and glass fibres can also be added to the mix for extra strength and durability. While stucco reliefs have been found on ancient Egyptian, Minoan, Etruscan, Mesopotamian and Persian buildings, stucco became particularly prevalent during the Renaissance, either smooth or textured, sometimes as decorative elements such as medallions and festoons. Stucco was also used to create opulent ornamentation for architecture during the Baroque period, while Neoclassical buildings regularly featured stucco on columns and entablatures. In the 1930s, International Style architecture was noted for its smooth, white stucco walls.

KEY DEVELOPMENTS

The elaborate curving, gilded and painted stucco inside the Wieskirche in Bavaria was created by the architect-artists Dominikus and Johann Baptist Zimmermann as a blend of fluid and flamboyant Rococo and Baroque styles. It conveys a sense of lightness, refinement and grandeur, symbolizing heaven and contrasting dramatically with the plain, undecorated exterior.

Wieskirche, Dominikus Zimmerman and Johann Baptist Zimmerman, 1745–54, Bavaria, Germany

RENAISSANCE **p.26** BAROQUE **p.29** ROCOCO **p.30** VILLA LA ROTONDA **p.96**
SAINT PAUL'S CATHEDRAL **p.106** WIESKIRCHE **p.108** CAPITOL BUILDING **p.112** VILLA SAVOYE **p.134**

Glass

KEY ARCHITECTS: JOSEPH PAXTON • LUDWIG MIES VAN DER ROHE • WALTER GROPIUS
CHARLES AND RAY EAMES • JUNYA ISHIGAMI • I. M. PEI

Eames House, Charles and Ray Eames, 1949, California, USA

KEY DEVELOPMENTS

Eames House, also known as Case Study House No. 8, was designed by husband-and-wife designers Charles (1907–78) and Ray Eames (1912–88) as their home and studio. It consists of two glass and steel rectangular boxes aligned along a central axis. Each is structured around a simple steel frame holding a wide variety of opaque and translucent panels.

Glass has been manufactured since at least 2500 BCE, and glass-blowing was discovered in the first century CE.

Glass was first used for windows by the ancient Romans, using cylindrical bubbles of glass that were sliced lengthwise and flattened. Windows remained small and scarce for the following centuries, but over time improvements in glass-making processes continued and windows became more common. In 1851 in London, Joseph Paxton (1803–65) designed the Crystal Palace, a huge glass and iron structure for the Great Exhibition made with hand-blown cylinder glass.

In 1952, British engineer and businessman Alastair Pilkington (1920–95) invented the float-glass process for commercial manufacturing of plate glass, which enabled glass to have a uniform thickness. From the early 1960s, all the world's leading flat-glass manufacturers obtained licences to use the Pilkington float-glass process, which supplanted all other methods to dominate the world market for high quality flat glass.

Glass and steel construction became a symbol of progress in the course of the twentieth century, and its use for curtain walls made buildings clad entirely in glass possible. Thanks to technical advances, many can now also incorporate large sheets of curved glass.

MODERNIST **p.37** BAUHAUS **p.43** HIGH-TECH **p.49** DOGE'S PALACE **p.86**
RIETVELD SCHRÖDER HOUSE **p.128** POMPIDOU CENTRE **p.150**

Stained Glass

KEY ARCHITECTS: ARNOLD OF NIJMEGEN • WILLIAM BURGES • LOUIS COMFORT TIFFANY
LLUÍS DOMÈNECH I MONTANER

Saint Vitus Cathedral, Matthias of Arras
and Peter Parler, 1344–97, building
continued intermittently until 1929,
Prague, Czech Republic

KEY DEVELOPMENTS
The vividly coloured, sparkling
stained-glass windows of Saint
Vitus Cathedral in Prague blend
religious history and powerful
human emotion, and range
from the huge, sumptuously
coloured rose window that
resembles the shape of the
Earth, to the richly designed
and coloured arched window
of the Schwarzenberg Chapel,
designed by Karel Svolinsky
(1896–1986) in 1929.

Coloured glass was produced by the ancient Egyptians, Phoenicians and Romans, with flourishing manufacture centres at Sidon, Tyre and Antioch during the first century CE.

Coloured glass was made by the addition of metallic salts or minerals during the fabrication process, and through Syrian merchants and sailors these methods circulated to China and Europe. At first, coloured glass was used in mosques, palaces and public buildings, but gradually its use in architecture dwindled.

Then, from the seventh century, Christian churches in Europe began to be built with windows made of tiny pieces of coloured glass held together by strips of lead. These stained-glass windows symbolized the jewelled walls of heaven described in the last book of the Bible, the Book of Revelation. Gothic churches began incorporating even larger stained-glass windows that illustrated Bible stories to communicate with the mainly illiterate worshippers. Increasingly wide and elaborate circular rose windows were constructed in French cathedrals in the twelfth and thirteenth centuries.

In 1893, Louis Comfort Tiffany (1848–1933) invented Favrile glass, an iridescent coloured glass used in the stained-glass windows of grand buildings during the Art Nouveau period.

GOTHIC **p.25** CHARTRES CATHEDRAL **p.78** SANTA MARIA DELLA FIORE **p.82** SAGRADA FAMÍLIA **p.120**

Iron

KEY ARCHITECTS: GUSTAVE EIFFEL • CHARLES BARRY

Although iron had been used in architecture in China in the eighth century, it was not until the eighteenth century that its use became extensive.

Strong, available in large quantities and relatively cheap, iron was employed in Europe for large-span supports in structures such as bridges and railway stations. For some considerable time, architects used iron to emulate historical façades, as it could be cast into numerous shapes and designs, creating elaborate façades that were far less costly than stone-carved examples. As it was strong enough to support heavy machinery, cast iron was also used for the structural elements of factories, although some early buildings collapsed when their brittle cast-iron beams fractured.

In an efficient, unprecedented manner, large iron structures could be prefabricated and transported across the world. Cast-iron columns were also slimmer than masonry columns, so could be both space-saving and elegant. Gradually, a new aesthetic emerged. In 1851, Joseph Paxton designed the Crystal Palace in London, a vast iron and glass structure that was imitated and adapted around the world.

KEY DEVELOPMENTS
Built as a temporary installation for the Exposition Universelle of 1889, the Eiffel Tower, designed by Gustave Eiffel (1832–1923), became an immediate sensation for its unprecedented appearance and extraordinary height. Mainly composed of wrought-iron in an open-lattice design, it consists of four massive arched legs set on masonry piers that curve in to meet as a single, tapering tower.

Eiffel Tower, Gustave Eiffel, 1887–9, Paris, France

GOTHIC REVIVAL **p.32** PALACE OF WESTMINSTER **p.114** KARLSPLATZ UNDERGROUND STATION **p.124**

Steel

KEY ARCHITECTS: LOUIS SULLIVAN • WILLIAM LE BARON JENNEY • I. M. PEI • ZAHA HADID
FRANK GEHRY • MOSHE SAFDIE • NORMAN FOSTER • BRUCE PRICE

In the late nineteenth century, iron was largely replaced by steel, which is more pliable, more uniformly strong, and has a high resistance to stress.

An alloy of iron, carbon and other elements, steel has a high tensile strength and is cheap to produce. Although evidence of its production has been found in Anatolia as early as c.1800 BCE, it was not until the mid-nineteenth century that steel was produced in large enough quantities to be used for building. In 1855, English inventor Henry Bessemer (1813–98) created the first inexpensive industrial process for the mass production of steel.

Gradually steel replaced iron in many architectural situations. Its first major use was for bridges. As it was so strong, steel was also used for open-plan interiors and high-rise buildings, and was to become essential in the development of the skyscraper. One of the first entirely steel-framed buildings was the American Surety Building in New York (1894–6) designed by Bruce Price (1845–1903). The Pompidou Centre in Paris was also built with a massive exterior steel frame, and its interior is spanned by huge steel trusses.

KEY DEVELOPMENTS
After German reunification in 1990, Norman Foster rebuilt the Reichstag in Berlin. To symbolize Germany's unity, democracy and freedom, he topped the design with a new steel and glass dome that gives a panoramic view of the surrounding city and also allows viewers to look down into the debating chamber of the Bundestag.

Reichstag, Paul Wallot, 1884–94, and Norman Foster, 1995–9, Berlin, Germany

CHICAGO SCHOOL **p.34** HIGH-TECH **p.49** WAINWRIGHT BUILDING **p.122** BAUHAUS BUILDING **p.130**
CHRYSLER BUILDING **p.132** SEAGRAM BUILDING **p.140** POMPIDOU CENTRE **p.150**

Aluminium

KEY ARCHITECTS: OTTO WAGNER • FRANK LLOYD WRIGHT • LUDWIG MIES VAN DER ROHE
EERO SAARINEN • RICHARD NEUTRA

Dymaxion House, Buckminster Fuller, 1948, Michigan, USA

KEY DEVELOPMENTS
In 1927, Buckminster Fuller designed a prefabricated house that weighed under three tonnes and could be built almost anywhere. The Dymaxion House was to have been available in several versions in factory-manufactured kits and assembled on site. Two prototypes were produced after World War II, and were eventually combined to build the only surviving example.

Strong, lightweight, durable, resistant to corrosion and able to be formed into many shapes, aluminium is also an easily recyclable material.

It was not until the end of the nineteenth century that an affordable method of extracting the metal from its ore bauxite was discovered, and not until the 1920s that it could be obtained cheaply and in bulk. Then, aluminium finally became practical for architects to use as its availability increased and costs came down.

The first well-known use of aluminium in a work of architecture was in the Empire State Building (1929–31) in New York City (see page 44), especially for its famous spire. Aluminium soon began to be used for building components such as beams, window and door frames, and particularly for façades and curtain walls. Aluminium alloys are now used to support heavy sheets of glass in numerous buildings.

Commerzbank Tower (1994–7) in Frankfurt, Germany, by Norman Foster is one of the tallest buildings in Europe, and is constructed with anodized aluminium panels on its exterior as rain screens, while extruded aluminium assists its ventilation. Although it remains more expensive than steel, many skyscrapers have aluminium frames, which enables them to become taller and more energy-efficient than ever.

ART DECO **p.44** CHRYSLER BUILDING **p.132**

Plastic

KEY ARCHITECTS: PETER COOK • COLIN FOURNIER • NICHOLAS GRIMSHAW • LI XINGGANG
CHRIS BOSSE

Eden Project, Nicholas Grimshaw,
1998–2001, Cornwall, UK

KEY DEVELOPMENTS

Hexagonal and pentagonal cells of ETFE plastic were made for the two steel-framed geodesic conservatories or 'biomes' that make up the Eden Project in Cornwall. Easily replaced, the cells serve to create environments that simulate a tropical rainforest in one dome and a Mediterranean climate in the other. Each dome houses thousands of thriving plant species.

Hard-wearing, adaptable and lightweight, plastics and polymers are among the most recent synthetic materials to be used extensively in architecture.

The first semi-synthetic plastics were developed in the mid-nineteenth century, but their use remained limited. Just before World War II, acrylic, polythene, PVC, polystyrene and nylon were introduced, but were rarely used in building until the 1970s when quality improved enough to make their use practicable, and it was also being discovered that some helped to save energy and reduce costs. For instance, the biomorphic Kunsthaus Graz in Austria (2001–03) by Peter Cook (b.1936) and Colin Fournier (b.1944) is covered with a semi-transparent skin of iridescent blue acrylic plastic that allows for built-in photovoltaic panels.

ETFE (ethylene tetrafluoroethylene) is a particularly strong polymer with a high resistance to weathering. Lightweight, durable and versatile, it has been used in many projects, including Beijing's National Stadium (2003–08) by Herzog & de Meuron and Ai Weiwei, and the city's National Aquatic Centre (2004–07) by PTW Architects. Red ETFE cushions were used between the 'twigs' at the National Stadium, while the National Aquatic Centre is the largest ETFE-clad structure in the world.

MONTREAL BIOSPHERE **p.148**

Carbon Fibre

KEY ARCHITECTS: ACHIM MENGES • MORITZ DÖRSTELMANN • MARIA YABLONINA

Strong and lightweight, carbon fibre consists of thin filaments of carbon bound together with plastic polymer resin by heat, by pressure or in a vacuum.

Lighter than steel yet five times stronger, twice as rigid and weighing considerably less, carbon fibre is a relatively new material. It was first produced in the late nineteenth century when inventors including Joseph Swan (1828–1914) and Thomas Edison (1847–1931) carbonized cotton and bamboo to make filaments for early incandescent light bulbs. Gradually its use expanded, but it was not until the early twenty-first century that carbon fibre was produced in large enough quantities and at a low enough price to be used in architecture.

Now often incorporated into reinforced concrete, cement and other materials, carbon fibre has reached the point where it is less expensive than many other building materials. Currently, however, many architects tend to use carbon fibre simply to mimic established architectural materials, much as iron was used at the end of the nineteenth century. As confidence grows – as happened with iron – it will be used in more innovative ways.

KEY DEVELOPMENTS
Following the design of the filament structures of the shells, or elytra, of flying beetles, the Elytra Filament Pavilion is made of exposed glass and carbon fibre. Each component was created by a robot at the University of Stuttgart, and the resulting filament structure is strong and light, spanning over 200 sq m (2,100 sq ft) yet weighing less than 2.5 tonnes.

Elytra Filament Pavilion, Achim Menges, Moritz Dörstelmann, Jan Knippers and Thomas Auer, 2016, London, UK

HIGH-TECH **p.49**

Recycled Materials

KEY ARCHITECTS: RENZO PIANO • NORMAN FOSTER • BILL DUNSTER • JAN JONGERT
WANG SHU • FAHED MAJEED

Recycling or using salvaged materials in architecture reduces waste, saves money and has a positive environmental impact.

Recycling has occurred in architecture for centuries, as valued building elements such as bricks, tiles and decorative items are recovered and re-used. However, since the late twentieth century, greater emphasis has been put on the importance of reusing building materials, and it often produces innovative, effective and artistic expressions of sustainable design.

Incorporating recycling into architectural design has become common during this 'green revolution', with elements such as wood, bricks, tiles and glass, as well as more unexpected materials such as bottles, ring-pull cans and rubber tyres, used in construction. One example is the durable houses by engineer Tateh Lehbib Braica in Yelwa, Nigeria, made of used plastic bottles filled with sand and secured with mud. In using materials that have previously had another purpose, energy requirements and emissions are reduced. 'Creative re-use' is a form of recycling in which entire buildings are re-purposed for uses that were not part of the original function.

KEY DEVELOPMENTS
Winner of the Pritzker Prize in 2012, Wang Shu (b.1963) designed Ningbo Museum using locally recovered materials, such as bamboo, tiles and bricks, some of them centuries old. Inside, each floor is different. For instance, the tilting second floor creates the forms of a mountain and a boat, suggesting the locality as well as the importance of Ningbo's sea-trading history.

Ningbo Museum, Wang Shu, 2007–08, Zhejiang Province, China

SUSTAINABLE **p.50** BOSCO VERTICALE **p.158**

Composite Materials

KEY ARCHITECTS: I. M. PEI • ZAHA HADID • KENGO KUMA • DAVID ADJAYE

Heydar Aliyev Cultural Center, Zaha Hadid, 2007–12, Baku, Azerbaijan

Mud-bricks and concrete are two of the oldest composites used in architecture. Several more have been invented from the late twentieth century on.

With its cellulose fibres bonded together by lignin, wood is an example of a natural composite, and engineered wood such as plywood builds on this strength, but is made to meet different needs. When iron-reinforced concrete was first invented, its strength and versatility revolutionized architecture. Since then, concrete has been reinforced with various materials, including steel rebar (an abbreviation of 'reinforcing bar') and synthetic or natural fibres.

Recent composite building materials are often durable, lightweight, non-corrosive and easily maintained. Some meet the exact requirements of a particular application, but the drawback of this is usually expense. However, fibreglass and some engineered laminates can suit a diversity of applications. Fibre-reinforced polymer (FRP) is particularly multi-faceted, made by combining a polymer resin with glass or carbon fibres. Strong, durable, waterproof and versatile, it was used by the design practice Snøhetta for the façade of SFMOMA (2010–16) in San Francisco.

KEY DEVELOPMENTS

The Heydar Aliyev Cultural Center in Azerbaijan is formed from an undulating curve that envelops the building. Mainly built with reinforced concrete, steel frames and composite beams and decks, it is entirely clad in white, smooth, strong glass-fibre-reinforced plastic (GFRP), a material that enables the building's curving, sinuous shapes, makes it easy to maintain and gives it longevity.

MODERNIST **p.37** HIGH-TECH **p.49** HABITAT 67 **p.146** POMPIDOU CENTRE **p.150**

Titanium

KEY ARCHITECTS: FRANK GEHRY • PAUL ANDREU • DANIEL LIBESKIND

Guggenheim Museum, Frank Gehry, 1992–7, Bilbao, Spain

In addition to being light, strong and durable, titanium is an excellent insulator, which means it can increase a building's energy efficiency.

Widely used in various building types such as museums, temples and shrines, as well as in housing, titanium has been exploited by architects since the 1970s. Its excellent corrosion-resistance properties can make certain architectural designs possible in the difficult, salty atmospheres of coastal areas, while its resistance to shock makes it suitable for earthquake-prone locations. Immune to many environmental pollutants, it is reliable and tough, and as an abundant and recyclable product, it is considered environmentally friendly.

Another positive for titanium's use in architecture is its strong reaction to oxygen. When exposed to moisture or air, an oxide film forms over titanium spontaneously, which protects it and means that it does not require a corrosion-preventive coating. Using this capability, from 2001 to 2007 Paul Andreu (1938–2018) designed the Beijing National Centre for the Performing Arts as a titanium and glass ellipsoid dome in the centre of an artificial lake, intended to resemble a water droplet, or an egg floating on water.

KEY DEVELOPMENTS

Canadian-American architect Frank Gehry chose 33,000 extremely thin titanium sheets for the cladding of the Guggenheim Museum in Bilbao after studying a sample of the metal pinned outside his office. Combined with limestone and glass, the museum's curved shell resembles a boat, evoking Bilbao's history and, depending on the weather and time of day, it changes colour.

HIGH-TECH **p.49** DECONSTRUCTIVIST **p.51**

Glossary

Adhisthana The raised base of a Buddhist or Hindu temple.

Ambulatory Aisles around the apse of a church, often with small chapels leading off.

Anta A pillar that stands on either side of the entrance of a Greek temple; also called *parasta*.

Apse Semi-circular or polygonal end of a church, usually at the end of the chancel.

Arcade A series of arches supported by columns or pillars; also a covered passage.

Architrave A horizontal beam supported by columns; the lowest part of an entablature.

Ardhamandapa A half-pavilion, usually found in front of or in place of the vestibule (*antarala*) of a Hindu temple, closed on two sides and open at the front.

Baldachin A canopy over an altar or throne; also called baldacchino.

Baluster A vertical supporting element, usually a small column or pillar.

Balustrade A row of balusters supporting a rail.

Baptistery A part of a church or a separate building near a church in which baptismal rites are performed.

Barrel vault The simplest form of vault, resembling a barrel or tunnel cut in half lengthways; also called tunnel or wagon vault.

Basilica A rectangular medieval church in which the nave is taller than the aisles, based on the Roman assembly hall.

Bond Brickwork laid with overlapping bricks.

Buttress Projecting masonry or brickwork that supports a wall; flying buttresses are arches or half-arches that push back against a building's outward thrust.

Campanile An Italian bell tower, usually separate from the church.

Cantilever A beam or balcony supported or fixed at one end, carrying a load at the other.

Capital The top of a column, pilaster or pier, usually beneath a lintel, entablature or arcade.

Casement window A frame that is hinged on one vertical side, which opens sideways.

Castellated Finished with turrets and battlements.

Cavetto Concave moulding, usually approximating a quarter circle.

Cella The inner chamber of a classical temple, or of a shop in domestic Roman architecture; also called *naos*.

Chaitya A Buddhist shrine or prayer hall with a stupa at one end; also called *chaitya-griha*.

Chatra A central pillar supporting a triple-umbrella form over a temple, representing the Three Jewels, or Triantha, of Buddhism; also called *chhatra* or *chattra*.

Chinoiserie The imitation of Chinese styles, popular in Europe during the 17th and 18th centuries.

Clerestory The upper storey of the nave of a church, pierced with windows.

Colonnade A range of columns that supports a string of continuous arches or a horizontal entablature.

Corbel A structural piece of stone, wood or metal extending from a wall, serving as a bracket.

Cornice A horizontal projecting moulding, often at the top of an entablature.

Crenellation Alternating raised and lowered wall sections at the top of a high wall, usually on castles for defensive purposes; also called battlement.

Crossing The area where the nave and transept intersect in a church, often topped by a tower, spire or dome.

Cupola A small dome or a hexagonal or octagonal tower at the top of a building, usually created to provide light and air or as a lookout. A belvedere is a square-shaped cupola.

Curtain wall A non-load-bearing wall, often made of glass. Alternatively, the outer wall of a castle.

Entablature The upper part of a classical order, above the column and capital.

Entasis A slight convex curve in the middle of a column or spire to counteract the optical illusion of indentation or narrowing.

Façade The exterior wall of a building, usually referring to the front face.

Frieze A band of sculpted ornamentation on a building, often the middle part of an entablature.

Fusuma Vertical rectangular panels in traditional Japanese architecture that slide sideways to open or close spaces.

Gable The triangular pointed portion of wall under a pitched roof, sometimes extended for decorative purposes.

Garbhagriha The innermost sanctum of a Hindu temple.

Gopuram A monumental gatehouse tower, usually ornate, at the entrance of certain Hindu temples in southern India; also called *gopura*.

Groin vaults Two barrel vaults that intersect at right angles.

Hammerbeam roof A decorative, open timber roof truss popular in England during the Gothic era.

Hanok A traditional Korean house, first designed and built in the 14th century.

Hipped roof A roof that is pitched at the ends as well as the sides.

Hypostyle A hall with a roof supported by multiple columns.

Keystone A wedge-shaped stone in the apex of an arch or vault that holds the other stones in place.

Lantern A cylindrical or polygonal structure with windows that tops a dome; its base is usually open to allow light to enter the area below.

Lintel A horizontal beam over a window or door opening that carries the weight of the wall.

Loggia A gallery formed by a colonnade, open on one or more sides.

Machicolation An opening between supporting corbels of a battlement, used for defensive purposes.

Mansard roof A roof with four sloping sides, each becoming steeper halfway down.

Mihrab The semi-circular niche in the wall of a mosque that indicates the direction of prayer.

Minaret A tall spire often with a conical or onion-shaped crown on or near a mosque, used to call the faithful to prayer.

Mullion Vertical bar between the panes of glass in a window.

Narthex A colonnaded porch in front of the façade of a church; alternatively, a transverse antechamber inside a church, before the nave and aisles.

Oculus A circular opening in the centre of a dome, such as the one in the roof of the Pantheon, Rome.

Ogee arch A pointed arch with an s-shaped curve on each side.

Order A classical style of architecture defined by a type of column. The three primary orders in ancient Greece and Rome were, in chronological order, Doric, Ionic and Corinthian.

Oriel A projecting window of an upper floor, supported from below by a bracket.

Pagoda A tiered tower with multiple roof layers, constructed around a central axis pole, found mainly in China, Japan and Korea.

Parapet A low protective wall located above any sudden drop, such as at the top of a façade.

Pediment A decorative triangular element over a portico.

Pendentive A curved, triangular piece of masonry that allows circular domes to be placed on square or polygonal structures beneath.

Pilaster A shallow, non-structural rectangular column, attached to, and projecting slightly from, a wall surface.

Pillar A structural support, similar to a column, but larger and often without ornamentation.

Piloti A pillar, column or stilt that supports a building, popularized by Le Corbusier and prevalent in International Style architecture.

Portico An entrance porch with columns or pilasters and a roof, often topped by a triangular pediment.

Pylon A support structure for suspension bridges or motorways; also a monumental gateway to ancient Egyptian temples.

Quatrefoil Ornamental design, often used in window tracery, of four leaves, resembling a flower or clover leaf; a trefoil is composed of three leaves.

Serlian window An arched window flanked by two shorter, non-arched windows, popularized by Palladio.

Shikhara A spire on a Hindu temple; also known as *vimana*.

Shoji In Japanese architecture, a sliding outer door and window made of a latticework wooden frame and covered with a tough, translucent white paper.

Spire A slender, pointed construction on top of a building, often a church.

Squinch A straight or arched structure across an interior angle of a square tower that carries a superstructure such as a dome.

Stupa A Buddhist commemorative monument usually housing sacred relics associated with the Buddha.

Tracery The stonework elements that support the glass in Gothic windows.

Transom A horizontal beam across an opening, often a door with a window above, hence transom window.

Trencadís A type of mosaic created from broken tiles and other ceramics, popular in Catalan Modernism.

Triforium A gallery or arcade above the arches of the nave, choir and transepts of a church.

Truss A rigid framework of wooden beams or metal bars that supports a structure, such as a roof.

Tuff A type of rock made of volcanic ash.

Turret A small tower that pierces a roof line, usually cylindrical and topped by a conical roof.

Vernacular architecture A style of architecture that uses local materials to create structures influenced by traditional designs.

Vihara A Buddhist monastery; its original meaning is 'a secluded place in which to walk'.

Voussoir A wedge-shaped stone in an arch or vault, the most prominent ones being the keystone and the springer (the bottom stone on each side of an arch).

Westwork The monumental, west-facing entrance section of a Carolingian, Ottonian or Romanesque church.

Zellige Mosaic tilework made from individually chiselled geometric tiles set into a plaster base, widely produced in Morocco.

Index

Illustrations are indicated in *italic*
Main entries are indicated in **bold**

A
Aalto, Alvar 7, 143
abbeys 24, *24*, 25, 72, *73*
Adam, Robert 31, 175, 186, 187,
203, 205
Adams, John 177
adhisthana 19, 216
Adjaye, David 214
Adler, Dankmar 34; Wainwright
Building *52*, **122–3**
adobe *see* mud-bricks
Aelius Nicon 14
Agra: Taj Mahal (Lahori) 8, 20, 27,
98–9, 200, *200*
Alberti, Leon Battista 26
Alfeld: Fagus Factory (Gropius and
Meyer) 37, *37*
aluminium 44, 49, 68, **210**
Ambrogio, Giovanni d' 82
Amenhotemp (son of Hapu) 12
Amsterdam 179, *179*; WoZoCo
(MVRDV) 189, *189*
Andernach: Maria Laach Abbey 24,
72–3
Ando, Tadao 48; Himeji City Museum
of Literature 201, *201*
Andreu, Paul 215
Angkor Wat *see* Siem Reap
Antelami, Benedetto 24, 72
Anthemius of Tralles: Hagia Sophia
17, *17*, 63
aqueducts 13, 16, *16*, 171, 173
arcades 16, 78, **171**, 216, 217; *see also*
colonnades
arches 20, 166, **173**; crenelated 22;
horseshoe 20, 22; lancet 22; ogee 22,
86, 217; perpendicular 24; pointed
25, 32, 77, 166, 171, 183; quatrefoil
20, 86; rounded 16, 24; trefoil 20, 86;
triumphal 16
Arnold of Nijmegen 207
Arnoldi, Alberto 82
Arnolfo di Cambio 25, 82
Arolat, Emre 185
Art Deco (style) **44**, 132
Art Nouveau (style) **36**, 37, 124–5,
180, *180*, 206
Arts and Crafts (style) **35**, 36, 37, 114,
116–17, 164, 168
Ashbee, C. R. 35
Asmara, Fiat Tagliero building 189
Aspdin, Joseph 205
asphalt *see* bitumen
Asplund, Hans 46
Assyrian civilization 187, 192, 194
Astras 17
Aswan: Abu Simbel Temple 12, *12*
asymmetry 30, 35, 36, 37, 41

Athens: Acropolis 14, 56–7;
Hephaestus, Temple of *14*;
Parthenon (Ictinus, Callikrates and
Phidias) 14, **56–7**, 200
Atik Sinan 20
atria 24, 38, 49, 72, **180**
Auer, Thomas: Elytra Filament
Pavilion 212, *212*

B
Babylon 187, 194
Bacon, Henry 200
Baeza, Alberto Campo 48
Bahá'í religion 40, *40*
Baillie Scott, M. H. 35
Baku: Heydar Aliyev Cultural Center
(Hadid) 214, *214*
balconies 30, *30*, 138, **170**; *see also*
galleries
baldachin/baldacchino 29, 216
balustrade 170, 216
Bam, Iran 193
bamboo 50, **199**, 202, 213
Ban, Shigeru 165, 196; Paper Log
Houses 197
Barcelona: Bac de Roda Bridge
(Calatrava) 38; Casa Batlló (Gaudí)
168, *168*, 170; Casa Milà (Gaudí) 36,
36, 169; Sagrada Família (Gaudí) 8,
120–1, 182, *182*, 184
Barma 195; Saint Basil's Cathedral 8,
17, **94–5**
Baroque (style) **29**, 32, *32*, 102, 106,
165, 171, 176, 183, 205, *205*
Barragán, Luis 48, 198
Barreca, Gianandrea 158
Barry, Charles 114, 164, 180, 195,
208; Palace of Westminster 32,
114–15, 184
basilicas 82, 182, 204, 216; *see also*
under individual entries
Batak architecture 199, *199*
Bauersfeld, Walther 45
Bauhaus (style) 37, 41, 42, **43**, 48,
130–1, 168
Bavaria: Neuschwanstein Castle
(Riedel and Dollmann) **118–19**;
Wieskirche (Zimmermann and
Zimmermann) 30, **108–9**, 181,
205, *205*
Behrens, Peter: AEG Turbine Hall 37
Beijing: Forbidden City 187, 198;
National Aquatic Centre (PTW
Architects) 211; National Centre for
the Performing Arts (Andreu) 215;
National Stadium (Herzog & De
Meuron and Ai Weiwei) 211
Berlage, Hendrik 41
Berlin: AEG Turbine Hall (Behrens)
37; Altes Museum (Schinkel) 31;
Brandenburg Gate (Langhans) 31;

Jewish Museum (Libeskind) 51, *51*;
Reichstag (Foster) 209, *209*
Bernini, Gian Lorenzo 171, 181, 182,
192; Saint Peter's 29
Bessemer, Henry 208
Bexleyheath: Red House (Webb and
Morris) 35, *35*, **116–17**
Bhubaneswar: Lingaraja Temple
21, *21*
Bilbao, Guggenheim Museum
(Gehry) 51, *190*, 215, *215*
bitumen **194**
Bo Bardi, Lina: São Paulo Museum of
Art 46, *46*
Böblinger, Matthäus 178
Boeri, Stefano 50, 158
Böhm, Dominikus 183
Bon, Bartolomeo 171, 192
Bon, Giovanni 171, 192
Borobudur, Java 15
Borromini, Francesco 29, 172, 182
Bosse, Chris 211
Bowellism 150; *see also* High-tech
(style)
Boyle, Richard: Chiswick House
28, *28*
Braica, Tateh Lehbib 213
Bramante, Donato: Belvedere Palace
176, *176*; Saint Peter's Basilica
29, **90–1**, 180, 192; Tempietto
(Bramante) 26, *26*
Brasilia, Cathedral (Niemeyer) **144–5**
Breuer, Marcel 43, 189
bricks 17, 32, 71, 164, 169, *169*, **195**,
213; *see also* mud-bricks
Brodsky, Alexander 197
Brunelleschi, Filippo; San Lorenzo,
Church of 90; Santa Maria del Fiore
8, 26, **82–5**, 172, *172*
Brutalist (style) 7, **46**
Bryce, David 32
Budapest, Széchenyi Thermal Bath
(Czigler) 165, *165*
Buddhist (style) **15**, 23
Buonvicino, Ambrogio 170
Burges, William 207
Büring, Johann Gottfried: Chinese
House 30
Burnett, Micajah: Centre Family
Dwelling House, Pleasant Hill 33, *33*
Burnham, Daniel 34; Monadnock
Building 195
buttresses 29, **178**, 216; flying 25, 78,
79, 178, *178*
byobu (folding screens) 18
Byzantine (style) **17**, 24, *62*, 63, 68, 86,
167, 172, 178, 204

C
Calatrava, Santiago 49, 174, 201; Bac
de Roda Bridge 38

Calendario, Filippo: Doge's Palace **86–7**, 171, *171*
calligraphy 20, 27
Callikrates: Parthenon 14, **56–7**, 200
Callinicus 17
Cameron, Charles: Pavlovsk Palace 31
campanili (bell towers) 29, *82*, 83, 216
Campbell, Colen 28
Campen, Jacob van 200
cantilevers 49, 138, 170, **189**, 216
'Capability' Brown, Lancelot: Croome
    Court 186, *186*
capitals (column) 24, 177, 216
carbon fibre 50, **212**
Casagrande, Marco 199
Casey, Thomas Lincoln 200
cast iron 32, 34, 113, 208
castles 174, 176; European 76–7, *76*,
    118, *119*; Japanese 18
cathedrals *see* churches/cathedrals *and
    under individual entries*
ceilings **165**, 181; trompe-l' œil 29, 109
cella 56, 60, 216
chaityas 15, 216
Chambiges, Pierre 203
Chanut, Ferdinand: Galeries Lafayette
    180, *180*
Charlottesville, Virginia: Rotunda
    (Jefferson) 31, *31*
Chartres Cathedral 25, *25*, **78–9**, 184
chatra 58, 59, 216
Chedanne, Georges: Galeries Lafayette
    180, *180*
Chelles, Jean de 25, 166
Chiang Rai: Wat Rong Khun (White
    Temple) (Kositpipat) 203, *203*
Chiattone, Mario 39
Chicago School (style) 7, **34**, 37
Chicago: Carson, Pirie, Scott and
    Company Building (Sullivan) 34, *34*;
    Home Insurance Building (Jenney)
    34; Monadnock Building (Burnham
    and Root) 195
chimneys 110, **169**
Chinoiserie 30, 216
churches/cathedrals 29, 182, 183;
    Baroque 29, *29*, 106, 109, 181, 205,
    205; Byzantine 17, *62*, 63, 167, 204,
    204; Gothic 25, 78, *79*, 82, 178, *178*,
    183, 184, 207; Renaissance 26, *26*,
    82–3, *82*, *83*, 84, 90, 91, 181; Rococo
    181, 205, *205*; Romanesque 24, *24*,
    72; Russian Orthodox 94, *95*
cities/towns 13, 14, 26, 39; *see also*
    urban planning
classical architectural styles/forms
    26, 28, 29, 31, 177; *see also* Greek,
    ancient; orders, classical; Roman,
    ancient
cloisters 18, 22, 171
colonnades 20, 22, 63, 68, 171, 106,
    216
columns 56–7, 86, 171, **177**, 186;
    Corinthian 14, 28, 60, 103, 177, 184;
    Doric 14, 56, 177; Ionic 14, 56, 177;

see also capitals (column); Hypostyle;
    piloti
composite materials 152, **214**, 172; *see
    also* concrete; mud-bricks
concrete 43, 46, 60, 154–5, 157, **201**,
    214; *see also* reinforced concrete
Constantinople 17, 20, 63; *see also*
    Istanbul
Cook, Peter: Kunsthaus Graz 211
corbels 77, 170, 178, 216
Cordoba: Great Mosque 22, *22*, 173
cornices 30, 33, 34, 110, 165, 216
Cornwall: Eden Project (Grimshaw)
    211, *211*
Cortona, Pietro 29
Coucy, Robert de 184
courtyards 22, 42, 81, **175**, 192
cruciform (building plan) 17, 25, 70,
    78, 90
Cullinan, Edward 196
Czigler, Győzo: Széchenyi Thermal
    Bath 165, *165*

D
Daumet, Honoré 203
De Stijl (style) **41**, 48, 128, 168
Deconstructivist (style) **51**, 154–5
Decrianus 16
Delacenserie, Louis 32
Delhi: Emperor Humayan's Tomb 27,
    98, 192; Lotus Temple (Sahba) 40, *40*
Della Porta, Giacomo 90
Dessau: Bauhaus Building (Gropius)
    130–1; Làzló Moholy-Nagy's House
    (Gropius) 43, *43*
deul/deula (tower) 21
Deutscher Werkbund 35, 37
Diotisalvi, Lanfranco 24; Leaning
    Tower of Pisa 174, *174*
Disch, Rolf 50
Djenné, Great Mosque (Traoré)
    126–7, 193, *193*
Doesburg, Theo van 41
Dollmann, Georg von:
    Neuschwanstein Castle (Riedel and
    Dollmann) **118–19**
Domènech i Montaner, Lluís 207
Domenico Da Cortona 169
domes 16, 60, 112–13, *192*; Baroque
    Baroque 29, *29*, 106, *106*; Byzantine
    17, *17*, *62*, 63; double 27; drum
    20; half 22, *83*; Islamic 20, 68, 185;
    onion-shaped 94, *95*, 98, *99*, 172;
    Palladian 28, *31*, 96, *96*; pointed 20;
    Renaissance 26, *26*, 82–3, *83*, 90, *91*,
    172, *172*; Roman, ancient 82–3; semi
    63; *see also* Geodesic (style)
doors **166**; sliding 18, 101, 196, 216
Dörstelmann, Moritz: Elytra Filament
    Pavilion 212, *212*
Dunster, Bill 213
Dur-Sharrukin 192
Dymaxion House (Fuller) 210, *210*

E
Eames, Charles and Ray: Eames House
    206, *206*
Eesteren, Cornelis van 41
Egyptian, ancient (style) 6, **12**, 54–5,
    166, 181, 198, 201, 203
Eiffel, Gustave: Eiffel Tower 174,
    208, *208*
Eisenman, Peter 51
Elliott + Associates 189
Endo, Arata 18
energy consumption 50, 196
energy efficiency 50, 158, 196, 215
entablature *26*, 109, 171, 186, 205, 216
entasis 56, 177, 216
environment *see* Sustainable (style)
Essen: Zollverein School of
    Management and Design (SANAA)
    10, 48, *48*
Expressionist (style) **40**

F
façades 30, 140, 150, 160, 208, 210, 216
Fahed Majeed 213
Federal style 33
Fernandes, Mateus 25
Fez: Dar al-Makhzen Royal Palace *162*,
    166, *166*
fibre-reinforced polymer (FRP) 214
Finsterlin, Hermann 40
Fioravante, Neri di 82
Fischer von Erlach, Johann Bernhard
    29
Fischer, Johann Michael 30
Flamboyant (Gothic style) 25, 78, 184
Flitcroft, Henry 28
Florence 26; Campanile (Giotto)
    82, 83; San Lorenzo, Church of
    (Brunelleschi) 90; Santa Maria
    del Fiore (Arnolfo di Cambio and
    Brunelleschi) 8, 26, **82–5**, 172, *172*
Florida, Spaceship Earth, EPCOT
    Center, Walt Disney World 45
Foster, Norman 150, 213;
    Commerzbank Tower 210; HSBC
    Building, Hong Kong 49, *49*;
    Reichstag 209, *209*
fountains 22, 47, *47*, 80, 81, 175
Fournier, Colin: Kunsthaus Graz 211
Frankfurt: Commerzbank Tower
    (Foster) 210
Frediani, Giovanni Battista: Saint Peter
    and Saint Paul's Church 181, *181*
Freed, Eric Corey 50
frieze 14, 56, 74, 122, 124, 152, 216
Fujisawa Sustainable Smart Town
    50, *50*
Fuller, Richard Buckminster 172;
    Dymaxion House 210, *210*; Montreal
    Biosphere 45, *45*, **148–9**
fusuma 18, 101, 196, 216
Futurist (style) **39**, 51, 144, 145, 189

G

gables 168, **179**, 216
Gabriel, Ange-Jacques 103
Gagini Family 186
Galizia, Emanuele Luigi 32
galleries 78, 86, 170, 185
garbhagriha 19, 216
gardens 22, 100, 134, 146, 158, 175
Garnier, Charles 194
gateways 19, 23, 59, 216
Gaudí, Antoni 174, 204; Casa Battló
168, *168*, 170; Casa Milà 36, *36*,
169; Sagrada Família 8, **120–1**, 182,
182, 184
Gehry, Frank 6, 209; Dancing House
51; Guggenheim Museum, Bilbao 51,
190, 215, *215*
Geodesic (style) **45**, 148–9, 172, 211, *211*
Gerhard of Cologne 178
Ghiberti, Lorenzo 166
Ghini, Giovanni di Lapo 82
Ghiyas, Mirak Mirza 27, 192
Gilbert Scott, George 32, 179
Gilbert, Cass: Woolworth Building 32
Giotto *82*, 83, 174
Girault, Charles 173
Giza: Great Pyramid 12, **54–5**, 192, *192*
glass 36, 42, 49, 160, 180, 187, 201,
206; curtain walls 130, 142, 164; *see
also* stained glass
Goff, Bruce 38
Goldfinger, Ernö 46
Goodrich, Daniel 33
gopurams 19, 216
gopuras 23
Gordon, Rodney 46
Gothic (style) **25**, 32, 72, 77, 82, 86,
86, 114, 165, 166, 168, 171, 173, 178,
178, 183, 207
Gothic Revival (style) 7, **32**, 36,
114–15, 116–17, 168, 179
Granada: Alhambra palace 22, *22*,
80–1, 167, *167*
Graves, Michael 47, 152
Gray, Eileen: Villa E-1027 42, *42*
Graz, Kunsthaus (Cook & Fournier) 211
Greek, ancient (style) 7, **14**, 31, 56–7,
166, 168, 177, 179, 181, 186, 187, 192,
200, 203
'green architecture' 50, 164; *see also*
Sustainable (style)
Grimshaw, Nicholas: Eden Project
211, *211*
Gropius, Walter 37, *37*, 43, 130, 206;
Bauhaus Building **130–1**; Fagus
Factory 37, *37*; Làzló Moholy-Nagy's
House 43, *43*
Guarini, Guarino 172
Gwynne, Patrick 188

H

Hadhramaut *see* Shibam Hadhramaut
Hadid, Zaha 8, 51, 201, 209; Heydar
Aliyev Cultural Center (Hadid) 214,
214; Vitra Fire Station **154–5**

Hadrami architecture *92*, 93
Hamburg: Elbphilharmonie (Herzog
& de Meuron) **160–1**
Hampton Court Palace 169, *169*
hanok 197, *197*, 216
Hardouin-Mansart, Jules 106, 165;
Versailles, Palace of **102–5**
Häring, Hugo 38
Haussmann, Georges-Eugène 164
Haywah, Raja ibn: Dome of the Rock
20, **68–9**, 204
Hébrard, Ernest 164
Helsinki Central Station (Saarinen)
164, *164*
Hemiunu 12
Heringer, Anna 199
Hermodorus of Salamis 16
Herzog & de Meuron: Beijing National
Stadium 211; Elbphilharmonie 160,
160, 176
High-tech (style) **49**, 150–1, 165
Himeji City Museum of Literature
(Ando) 201, *201*
Hindu (style) **19**, 23, 27, 70–1, *70*, 74
Hippodamus of Miletus 14
Hoban, James: White House 31,
177, *177*
Hoff, Robert van 't 41
Hoffmann, Josef 36
Höger, Fritz 40
Holabird, William 34
Hollein, Hans 47
Holzer, Michael 189
Homs: Krak des Chevaliers **76–7**
Hong Kong: HSBC Building (Foster)
49, *49*
Hopkins, Michael 49
Horta, Victor 36
Horyu-ji 18, *18*
Hospitaller Order of Saint John of
Jerusalem 76, 77
Howard, Thomas C. 45
Huguet 183
Hunt, Sumner 180
Hypostyle 20, 217

I

Ictinus: Parthenon 14, **56–7**, 200
Illinois, Farnsworth House (Mies van
der Rohe) 187, *187*
Imhotep 12
Inca architecture 88, *89*
Ineni 12
International Style 37, 41, **42**, 48, 135,
140, 167, 168, 187, *187*, 205
Iraq 20, *20*, 185; *see also* Mesopotamia
iron 36, 114, 201, **208**; *see also* cast iron
Ishigami, Junya 206
Isidore of Miletus: Hagia Sophia 17,
17, 63
Islamic (style) **20**, 22, 24, 27, 68, *68*, 76,
77, 80, *80*, 166, 167, 170, 175, 185, *185*
Istanbul: Blue Mosque 189, 198,
198; Hagia Sophia (Isidore and
Anthemius) 17, *17*, 20, **62–3**, 118
Iznik tiles 198, *198*

J

Japanese (style) **18**, 48, 166, 167
Java: Prambanan **70–1**
Jeanneret, Charles-Edouard *see* Le
Corbusier
Jeanneret, Pierre 134, 188, *188*; Villa
Savoye 42, **134–7**, 188, *188*
Jefferson, Thomas 112, 171, 186; Rotunda
31, *31*; White House 31, 177, *177*
Jenney, William Le Baron 209; Home
Insurance Building 34
Jerusalem: Dome of the Rock
(Haywah and Sallam) 20, **68–9**, 204
Johnson, Moses 33
Johnson, Philip 42, 47, 167, 187
Jones, Inigo 28, 106, 165
Jongert, Jan 213
Joy, William 178
Jujol i Gibert, Josep Maria 204

K

Kahn, Louis 38, 146, 195, 201
Kalinga (style) **21**
Karim, Mir Abdul 27
Karpion 14
Kent, William: Chiswick House 28, *28*
keystone 173, 217
Khan, Makramat 27
Khmer architecture 7, **23**, 74–5, *74*
Kihlberg, Carl 170
Klerk, Michel de 40
Knipper, Jan: Elytra Filament Pavilion
212, *212*
Kolkata: Dakshineswar Kali Temple
19, *19*, 184
Koolhaas, Rem 51
Korean architecture 15, 167, 197
Kositpipat, Chalermchai: Wat Rong
Khun (White Temple) 203, *203*
Krinsky, Vladimir 37
Kuma, Kengo 196, 199, 214
Kurokawa, Kisho 167

L

L'Enfant, Pierre Charles 112
La Città Nuova (Sant'Elia) 39, *39*
La Varra, Giovanni 158
Labrouste, Henri 37
Ladovsky, Nikolai 37
Lahore Fort, Pakistan 27, *27*
Lahori, Ustad Ahmad: Taj Mahal 8, 20,
27, **98–9**, 200, *200*
Lamb, William F.: Empire State
Building 44, *44*, 174, 210
Langhans, Carl Gotthard:
Brandenburg Gate 31
lath and plaster 183; *see also* plaster
Latrobe, Benjamin Henry 171; Capitol
Building 31, **112–13**; White House
31, 177, *177*
Le Corbusier 201, 205; Unité
d'Habitation 46; Villa Savoye 42,
134–7, 188, *188*
Le Vau, Louis: Versailles, Palace of **102–5**
Ledoux, Claude-Nicolas 31

Lethaby, William Richard 35
Li Xinggang 211
Libergier, Hugues 183, 184
Libeskind, Daniel 198, 215; Jewish
    Museum 51, *51*
Libon 14
limestone 12, 16, 55, 77, 93, 118, 192
loggia 170, 171, 217
London 28, 32, 47, 184; Chiswick
    House (Boyle and Kent) 28, *28*;
    Elytra Filament Pavilion (Menges,
    Dörstelmann, Knippers, Auer) 212,
    212; Palace of Westminster (Barry
    and Pugin) 32, **114–15**, 184; Saint
    Paul's Cathedral (Wren) **106–7**
Longhena, Baldassare 181; Santa
    Maria della Salute 29, *29*
Loos, Adolf 205; Steiner House 37
Lutyens, Edwin 173, 195

M
machicolations 77, 217
Machu Picchu: Temple of the Sun
    88–9
Maderno, Carlo 29, 182; Saint Peter's
    Basilica 90, 180
Maharashtra: Kailasanatha temple
    192
Maki, Fumihiko 18
Makovecz, Imre 38
Mandelstamm, Paul 170
Mannerist (style) 86
Mansart, François 168
marble 56, 71, *83*, 86, 98, *104*, **200**
Marchi, Virgilio 39
Marseilles, Unité d'Habitation
    (Le Corbusier) 46
Master Mateo 24, 72
Matsui, Yasuo 44
Matthias of Arras 25; Saint Vitus
    Cathedral 207, *207*
Mayan architecture 13, 64–5, *64*, *65*,
    66, 187
Mazzoni, Angiolo 39
McDonough, William 50
medieval architecture 32, 77, 114, 117,
    118, *119*, 165, 166, 167, 168, 170, 171,
    176, 203; *see also* Gothic (style)
Meem, John Gaw 193
Mehmed Agha, Sedefkar 20, 198
Meissonnier, Juste-Aurèle 30, 103
Mendelsohn, Erich: Einstein Tower 40
Menges, Achim: Elytra Filament
    Pavilion 212, *212*
Mesopotamia 6, 173, 178, 192, 193,
    194, *194*, 198, 204
Metabolism (Burnt Ash School) 18
Meuron, Pierre de *see* Herzog & de
    Meuron
Meyer, Adolf 130; Fagus Factory 37,
    37
Meyer, Hannes 43
Michelangelo Buonarroti 26, 176;
    Saint Peter's Basilica 29, **90–1**, 180, 192
Michelozzo 175

Mies van der Rohe, Ludwig 8, 43, 206,
    210; Farnsworth House 187, *187*;
    Seagram Building **140–1**
Milan: Bosco Verticale (Stefano Boeri
    Architetti) **158–9**
Milunić, Vlado: Dancing House 51
minarets 20, *20*, *62*, 63, 98, *99*, 126,
    170, **185**, 217
Minimalist (style) **48**, 130
Modernismo (style) 120
Modernist (style) 7, 18, **37**, 42, 43, 47,
    49, 135, 140, *141*, 164, 167, 168
Momo, Giuseppe 176
Monadnock Building (Burnham and
    Root) 195
Montreal: Biosphere (Fuller and Sadao)
    45, *45*, **148–9**; Habitat 67 (Safdie) **146–7**
Montreuil, Pierre de 166
Moore, Charles: Piazza d'Italia 47, *47*
Moorish (style) 7, 20, **22**, 175; *see also*
    Mudéjar architecture
Morris, William: Red House 35, *35*,
    116–17
mosaics 17, 27, 120, **204**
Moscow: Saint Basil's Cathedral
    (Barma and Yakovlev) 8, 17, **94–5**
mosques 20, *20*, *62*, 63, 80, 126–7, 167,
    171, 185, *185*
mouldings **181**
mud-bricks 12, *92*, 93, 126–7, **193**,
    194, 214
Mudéjar architecture 175, *175*
Mughal (style) **27**, 98
muqarnas 22
Murcutt, Glenn 50
MVRDV: WoZoCo 189, *189*

N
Nara: Todai-ji Temple 196, *196*
Nash, John 31, 164, 184, 187
naves **182**
Neo-Expressionism 40
Neoclassical (style) 7, **31**, 112–13, 172,
    177, *177*, 186, *186*, 205
Neutra, Richard 42, 210
New Orleans: Piazza d'Italia (Moore)
    47, *47*
New York 209: Chrysler Building
    (Van Alen) 8, **132–3**; Empire State
    Building, New York (Shreve, Lamb
    and Harmon) 44, *44*, 174, 210;
    Seagram Building (Mies van der
    Rohe) **140–1**; Woolworth Building
    (Gilbert) 32; World's Fair (1964) 45
Niemeyer, Oscar 39; Cathedral of
    Brasília **144–5**
Ningbo Museum (Wang Shu) 213,
    213
nipa huts (*bahay-kubo*) 199
Nishizawa, Ryue: Moriyama House
    156–7; Zollverein School of
    Management and Design *10*, 48, *48*
Nouvel, Jean 49

O
oculus 16, 60, 78, 90, 96, 112, 217
Oklahoma: POPS gas station 189
Oliveira, Mateus Vicente de 30
open-plan interiors 37, 42, 128, 134,
    150, 209
Orbais, Jean d' 178, 184
Orcagna, Andrea 82
orders, classical 14, 34, 56, 152, 177
Organic (style) **38**, 138
Otto, Frei 168
Oud, J. J. P. 41

P
pagodas 15, 18, 217
palaces 13, *13*, 20, 29, 86, *86*, 102–3,
    102, *103*, *104*, 171, *171*, 175, *175*, 187
Palenque 64; Palace of 13, *13*, 187;
    Temple of Inscriptions **64–7**
Palladian (style) **28**, 31, 186, *186*
Palladio, Andrea 26, 28, 31, 175, 177,
    186, 205; Doge's Palace **86–7**, 171,
    171; Villa La Rotonda **96–7**
Pandala, Eugene 50
panels *see* screens/panels
paper 101, 166, 167, **197**
Paper Log Houses (Ban) 197
Paris 36, 44; Eiffel Tower (Eiffel)
    174, 208, *208*; Galeries Lafayette
    (Chedanne and Chanut) 180, *180*;
    La Grande Arche de la Défense (Von
    Spreckelsen) 173, *173*; Panthéon
    (Saint Geneviève Church) (Soufflot)
    31; Pompidou Centre (Piano and
    Rogers) 49, **150–1**, 208; *see also*
    Versailles, Palace of
Parler, Heinrich 25
Parler, Peter 183; Saint Vitus Cathedral
    207, *207*
Parmenion 14
Pawson, John 48
Paxton, Joseph 206, 208
pediments 179, 217
Pei, I. M. 206, 209, 214
Pelz, Paul Johannes 165
pendentives 17, 22, 106, 217
Pennsylvania, Fallingwater (Wright)
    38, *38*, **138–9**, 189
Peralta 17
Peretti, Marianne 144
Perpendicular (Gothic style) 25
Perret, Auguste 37
Perriand, Charlotte 42, 168
Persian architecture 20, 27, 98
Petronas Kameteros 17
Pettazzi, Giuseppe 189
Pflüger, Conrad 25
Phaeax 14, 194
Phidias: Parthenon 14, **56–7**, 200
Philadelphia: Vanna Venturi House
    (Venturi and Scott Brown) 47
Piano, Renzo 213; Pompidou Centre
    49, **150–1**, 208
piers 24, 177; *see also* buttresses;
    columns

pilasters 103, 178, 186, 217
Pilkington, Alastair 206
pillars 38, 118, 176, 177, 217; *see also*
  columns; piloti
piloti 134, *134*, 135, **188**, 217
Pisa: Leaning Tower of (Diotisalvi and
  Pisano) 174, *174*
Pisano, Andrea 83; Leaning Tower of
  Pisa 174, *174*
plaster 17, 126, 183, 165, **203**
plastic 172, **211**
Poelzig, Hans 40
Poissy: Villa Savoye (Le Corbusier and
  Pierre Jeanneret) 42, **134–7**, 188, *188*
Pollodorus of Damascus 16
Pont du Gard 16, *16*
Ponte, Antonio da: Doge's Palace **86–7**,
  171, *171*
porticos/porches 28, 97, **186**, 217
Portland Building (Graves) **152–3**
post and beam *see* timber framing
Postmodern (style) 7, **47**, 51, 152–3
Potsdam: Chinese House (Büring) 30;
  Einstein Tower (Mendelsohn) 40
Prague: Dancing House (Gehry and
  Milunić) 51; Saint Vitus Cathedral
  (Matthias of Arras and Parler)
  207, *207*
Pre-Columbian (style) **13**, 65; *see also*
  Mayan architecture
precious/semi-precious stones 27,
  98, 200
Price, Bruce 209
Prix, Wolf D. 51, 189
pueblo architecture 193
Pugin, Augustus: Palace of
  Westminster 32, **114–15**, 184
pyramids: Egyptian 12, 54–5, 192, 198;
  Khmer 74; Mayan 64, *64*, *65*, *66*; Pre-
  Columbian Mesoamerican 13
Pytheos 192

Q

Quarenghi, Giacomo 31
quatrefoil (design) 20, 86, 217
Quimper Cathedral 178, *178*

R

Rabirius 16
Rapp, Isaac 193
Rastrelli, Francesco Bartolomeo:
  Catherine Palace 30, *30*
Ravenna: Church of San Vitale 17,
  204, *204*
Rechter, Zeev 188
recycled/recyclable materials 197, 210,
  213, 215
reinforced concrete 42, 130, 144, 145,
  146, 164, 176, 201, 212, 214, *214*
Reitzel, Erik 173
Renaissance (style) 7, **26**, 86, 165, 167,
  168, 176, *176*, 183, 187, 205
residential projects 128, 156–7,
  158–9, 160–1, 189, *189*; *see also under
  individual entries*

Riedel, Eduard: Neuschwanstein Castle
  (Riedel and Dollmann) **118–19**
Rietveld, Gerrit: Rietveld Schröder
  House 41, *41*, **128–9**
Rijke, Alex de 196
Rizzo, Antonio: Doge's Palace **86–7**,
  171, *171*
Robertson, Howard 44
Roche, Martin 34
Rococo (style) **30**, 36, 109, 165, 205, *205*
Rodia, Simon 204
Rogers, Richard: Pompidou Centre 49,
  150–1, 208
Roman, ancient (style) 7, **16**, 24, 26,
  31, 60–1, 82–3, 166, 171, 172, 173,
  176, 177, 180, 182, 183, 186, 187, 195,
  200, 201, 203, 204, 206
Romanesque (style) **24**, 72, 171
Rome 29; Belvedere Palace (Bramante)
  176, *176*; Colosseum 16, 26, 171, 192;
  Pantheon 16, 26, 31, **60–1**, 83, 97;
  Saint Peter's Basilica (Bramante and
  Michelangelo Buonarroti) 29, **90–1**,
  180, 192; Tempietto (Bramante) 26,
  26; Temple of Portunus 186
roofs **168**; flat 37, 41, 42, 43, 130,
  134, 168; gardens on 42, 134, *135*,
  146; hammerbeam 168, 196, 216;
  hip-and-gable *100*, 101; hipped 101,
  168, 217; irimoya 18, *18*; Mansard
  168, 217
Root, John: Monadnock Building 195
Roquebrune-Cap-Martin: Villa E-1027
  (Gray) 42, *42*
Rossi, Aldo 47
Rudolph, Paul 46, 188
Rufinus 17
Russian Orthodox architecture 94

S

Saarinen, Eero 164, 165, 173, 210
Saarinen, Eliel 165; Helsinki Central
  Station 164, *164*
Sabah: Kota Kinabalu City Mosque
  185, *185*
Sadao, Shoji: Montreal Biosphere 45,
  45, **148–9**
Safdie, Moshe 209; Montreal, Habitat
  67 146, *146*
Sahba, Fariborz 200: Lotus Temple
  40, *40*
Saint Petersburg: Pavlovsk Palace
  (Cameron) 31
Sallam, Yazid ibn: Dome of the Rock
  20, **68–9**, 204
Samarra: Great Mosque of al-
  Mutawakkil 20, *20*, 185
SANAA 157; Zollverein School of
  Management and Design 10, 48, *48*
Sanchi: Great Stupa 15, *15*, **58–9**
sandstone 21, 27, 65, 75, 192
Sangallo the Younger, Antonio da
  90, 176
Sant'Elia, Antonio: *La Città Nuova*
  39, *39*

Santos De Carvalho 173
São Paulo Museum of Art (Bardi)
  46, *46*
Saqqara: Djoser step pyramid 192, 198
Satyros 14
Scamozzi, Vincenzo 28, 96
Schindler, Rudolph 42
Schinkel, Karl Friedrich 167; Altes
  Museum 31
Schmidt, Friedrich: Vienna City Hall
  32, *32*
Schoenborn, August 112
Scott Brown, Denise: Vanna Venturi
  House 47
screens/panels 18, 128, 182, 197
Seagram Building (Mies van der
  Rohe) **140–1**
Sejima, Kazuyo 157; Zollverein School
  of Management and Design 10,
  48, *48*
Senenmut 12
Seoul: *hanok* 197, *197*
Severance, H. Craig 132
Severus 16
Seville: Alcázar 175, *175*
Shaker (style) **33**, 110–11; *see also*
  Shaker villages
Shaker villages: Hancock **110–11**;
  Pleasant Hill (Burnett and Johnson)
  33, *33*
Shanghai, Expo 2010 199
Shaw, Richard Norman 35
Shibam Hadhramaut **92–3**
shikhara (vimana) 19, 217
shoji 45, *45*, 175, 196, 217
Shreve, Lamb and Harmon: Empire
  State Building 44, *44*, 174, 210
shrines 12, 15, 18, 19, 21; Hindu 68, 75
Siem Reap: Angkor Wat 23, *23*, **74–5**
Silvestrin, Claudio 48
Sinan, Mimar 20, 185, 198
Sinan: Kota Kinabalu 18
skyscrapers 34, 39, 44, *44*, 122, 132,
  133, 140, 158–9, 174, 184, 201, 209,
  210; *see also under individual entries*
Smithson, Alison and Peter 46
Soane, John 31
Sone Tatsuzo 18
Soufflot, Jacques-Germain 186;
  Panthéon (Saint Geneviève Church)
  31
spires 25, 78, *79*, 174, **184**, 217
Sprecklesen, Johan Otto von: La
  Grande Arche de la Défense 173, *173*
squinches 17, 217
St Louis: Wainwright Building
  (Sullivan and Adler) *52*, **122–3**
stained glass 44, 78, 144, **207**
staircases **176**
Stam, Mart 43, 189
steel 42, 44, 132, 201, **209**; building
  frames 34, *34*, 45, 122, *123*, 124,
  132, 140, 148, 150, 164, 176, 206,
  206, 214
Stefano Boeri Architetti: Bosco
  Verticale **158–9**

Steiner, Rudolf 169
Stevenson, J. J. 179
stone 12, 44, 55, 71, 86, 88, 164, **192**, 201; *see also* limestone; sandstone
Stratford-upon-Avon: Shakespeare's Birthplace 202, *202*
Streamline Moderne 42, 44
Structural Expresssionism *See* High-tech (style)
stucco 30, *30*, 65, **205**
stupas 15, *15*, 19, 58–9, 217
Suger, Abbot 25
Sukiya 100–101, *100*
Sullivan, Louis 209; Carson, Pirie, Scott and Company Building (Sullivan) 34, *34*; Wainwright Building 52, **122–3**
Sumatra: Batak House 199, *199*
Sustainable (style) **50**, 158–9, 196, 213
Svolinsky, Karel 207
Sydney Opera House (Utzon) 38, **142–3**, 168
symmetry 12, 18, 27, 28, 127, 144

T
Tabassum, Marina 185
Takeda Ayasaburo 18
Takeru Shoji 175
Talenti, Francesco 82, 83
Talinn: Saint Olaf's Church 184, *184*
Tange, Kenzo 18
Tatsuno Kingo 18
Taut, Bruno 40
Teague, Walter 44
technology 36, 39, 50, 150; *see also* High-tech (style); Sustainable (style)
temples
   Bahá'í 40, *40*; Buddhist 15, 23, 74, 203, *203*; Egyptian, ancient 12, *12*; Greek, ancient 14, *14*, 56–7, 186, 187, 203; Hindu 19, *19*, 23, 70–1, *70*, 74, 192; Japanese 18, *18*, 196, *196*; Kalinga (India) 21, *21*; Khmer 23, *23*, 74–5, *74*; Mesopotamian 178; Pre-Columbian Mesoamerican 13, 64–5, *64*, *65*, 66, 88, *89*; Roman, ancient 16, 186, 187
Teotihuacan 13, 65
terraces 146–7, **187**
Testa, Clorindo 46
theatres 14, 170
Thornton, William: Capitol Building 31, **112–13**
Tiffany, Louis Comfort 207
tiles 22, 166, *166*, **198**, 213
timber framing 196
titanium **215**
Tokyo: Moriyama House (Nishizawa) **156–7**
tombs: Egyptian, ancient 6, 93, 166; Islamic 20; Mayan 64–5; Mughal 27, 98, *99*, 192; *see also* pyramids
towers 32, *32*, 72, *73*, 114, 158, **174**, 208, *208*; *see also* campanili

towns *see* cities/towns; urban planning
transom 101, 217
Traoré, Ismaila 193; Djenné Great Mosque 126, 127, 193, *193*
Trdat 17
trencadís 36, 204, 217
triforium (gallery/arcade) 78, 171, 217
trompe-l'œil (painting) 29, 30, 109
trusses 189, 209, 217
Tsarskoye Selo: Catherine Palace (Rastrelli) 30, *30*
Tschumi, Bernard 51
tuff (volcanic ash) 65, 90, 217
turrets 114, 118, 217
Twickenham, Strawberry Hill 32

U
Ur, Great Ziggurat of 194, *194*
urban planning 6, 14, 26, 31, 39
Ustad Isa Shirazi 20, 27
Utrecht: Rietveld Schröder House (Rietveld) 41, *41*, **128–9**
Utzon, Jørn: Sydney Opera House 38, **142–3**, 168

V
Van Alen, William 44, 166; Chrysler Building 8, **132–3**
Vanvitelli, Luigi 176
vaults/vaulting **183**; arching 25; barrel 24, 118, 183, 216; cross 16, 25; groin 24, 178, 183, 216; honeycomb/stalactite 22; pendentive 17, 63, 106; ribbed 25, 183, *183*
Velde, Henry van de 36
Venice 17, *195*; Doge's Palace (Calendario, Rizzo, Da Ponte and Palladio) 86–7, 171, *171*; Santa Maria della Salute (Longhena) 29, *29*
Venturi, Robert: Vanna Venturi House 47
verandas 18, 19
vernacular architecture/materials 35, 127, 217
Verona: Casa di Giulietta 170, *170*
Versailles, Palace of (Le Vau and Hardouin-Mansart) **102–5**
Vicenza: La Rotonda (Villa Almerico Capra) (Palladio) **96–7**
Vickers, Squire J. 204
Vienna Secession 124
Vienna: City Hall (Schmidt) 32, *32*; Karlsplatz Underground Station (Wagner) **124–5**; Steiner House (Loos) 37
vihara 15, 217
Viollet-Le-Duc, Eugène Emmanuel 32, 167
Vitruvius (Marcus Vitruvius Pollio) 28, 177, 194; *De Architectura* 6, 16, 26, 61
Vo Trong Nghia 199
voussoirs 173, 217
Voysey, C. F. A. 35, 179

W
Wagner, Otto 36, 210; Karlsplatz Underground Station **124–5**
Wallis, Thomas 44
Wallot, Paul: Reichstag 209, *209*
walls **164**; curtain 77, 130, 142, 206, 210, 216; glass 130, 142, 206
Walter, Thomas Ustick 172; Capitol Building 31, **112–13**
Wang Shu: Ningbo Museum 213, *213*
Washington, DC 200; Capitol Building (Thornton and Walter) 31, **112–13**; White House (Hoban, Jefferson and Latrobe) 31, 177, *177*
wattle and daub 164, **202**
Webb, Philip 179, 195; Red House 35, *35*, **116–17**
Weil-am-Rhein: Vitra Fire Station (Hadid) **154–5**
Wells Cathedral 183, *183*
westwork (church architecture) 72, 217
Wiener Werkstätte 37
Wils, Jan 43
windows 24, 43, 116, *167*, 206; arched 24, 207, *207*; casement 167, 216; clerestory 63, 78, 216; interior 110; lancet 32, 78; large 33, *33*, 34, *34*, 178; oculus 78; ribbon 49, 134, 135, *135*, 167, *188*; sash 167; serlian 28, 217; stained-glass 25, 116, 167, 207; tracery 25, 32, 217
Wittwer, Hans 43
wood 12, 18, 44, 50, 100, *100*, 101, 165, 166, **196**, 214
Wood the Younger, John 31
Worcestershire: Croome Court ('Capability' Brown) 186, *186*
Wren, Christopher 182; Saint Paul's Cathedral **106–7**
Wright, Frank Lloyd 6, 37, 41, 122, 175, 210; Fallingwater 38, *38*, **138–9**, 189
Wright, Tom 180
Wyatt, Matthew Digby 169
Wyman, George 180

X
Xiang, Kuai 166

Y
Yablonina, Maria 212
Yakovlev, Postnik 195; Saint Basil's Cathedral 8, 17, **94–5**
Yeang, Ken 50
Yokohama: Rinshunkaku **100–101**

Z
ziggurats 6, 194, *194*
Zimmermann, Dominikus and Johann 165; Wieskirche 30, **108–9**, 181, 205, *205*
Zaor, Jan: Saint Peter and Saint Paul's Church 181, *181*

Picture Credits